Social Me___

Marketing Strategies For Rapid Growth Using:
Facebook, Twitter, Instagram, LinkedIn, Pinterest And YouTube

By John Williams

Table of Contents

Introduction

Marketing. So much comes to mind with that one word. No business can survive without it, yet it's hard to keep up with changing trends – and yes, the trends have changed drastically, particularly in the past 10 years. First, I'll talk about what hasn't changed when it comes to marketing your business – your unique selling proposition. In other words, you need to have a unique position in the marketplace from which to promote your business and its products and/or services. And not only is this still a requirement in marketing, it's more important than ever before because you are no longer just competing against local business; you are competing on a global scale.

Is there any other aspect of marketing that hasn't changed? Nope.

That leaves us to discuss everything that has changed in marketing, which is a heck of a lot. Let's take a short look at the changes. The first thing that comes to mind is technology and this is absolutely the biggest change in marketing. Changes in technology have fueled significant changes in the marketing industry. We no longer just have radio, television, and print as forms of advertising. Businesses no longer have to rely on big ad agencies to get the word out about what they have to offer. The Internet and smart devices have opened up a whole new realm of marketing that is ripe for the picking.

Social Media Marketing

"Social media is not just an activity; it is an investment of valuable time and resources. Surround yourself with people who not just support you and stay with you, but inform your thinking about ways to WOW your online presence."
Sean Gardner

Social Media Marketing (SMM) is one aspect of that greater realm of today's marketing. To understand SMM, you must first have a solid understanding of what social media is. When we think of traditional forms of media, we generally think of television, radio, newspapers, and magazines. With these forms of media, communication flows in one direction, from the initiator of the communication to the recipient. Social media is media in which the communication goes two ways, back and forth, between the two communicators. There are numerous forms of social media, including:

- Blogging
- Forums
- Social networks (Facebook, Twitter, LinkedIn)
- Media-sharing sites (YouTube, Instagram)
- Social bookmarking and voting sites (Reddit, Digg)
- Review sites (Yelp)
- Virtual worlds (Second Life)

SMM is the focus of this book because of the incredible power it represents. Simply put, SMM is a method of marketing that taps into social media websites to represent your brand and bring traffic to your website and attention to your products and services.

In order to take full advantage of SMM, you must dive in headfirst. This means getting rid of potential assumptions you might be harboring. Here are two potential assumptions you might have regarding SMM:

- Social media is a fad – it's not and it's not going anywhere.
- Social media is about money or business – it's not; it's about the average person.

If you make either or both of these assumptions, this decision will ruin your chances of marketing via social media before you even get started.

Is SMM Really that Important?

"I use social media as an idea generator, trend mapper and strategic compass for all of our online business ventures."
Paul Barron

If you are asking that question, then thank goodness you are reading this book! Yes! Social media is perhaps the most important media for marketing that has ever existed. SMM is about connecting directly with the consumer (we'll talk more about that later).

There is nothing more powerful than connecting directly with the consumer. Nothing.

According to the Pew Research Center's research on social networking, as of January 2014 74% of adults who were online were using social networking sites. In terms of age groups, 89% of people between 18 and 29 and 82% of people between the ages of 30 and 49 were using social media. In terms of gender, 72% of men and 76% of women were using social networking sites.

Of course, this means that you had better know how to carry a conversation, and if you don't, then you had better learn how to in a hurry. You will be talking with consumers via the internet every day, because as of September 2014, the breakdown of the percentage of online adults using each of the major social networking sites was as follows:

- 71% of online adults use Facebook
- 23% of online adults use Twitter

- 26% use Instagram
- 28% use Pinterest
- 28% use LinkedIn

More recent global statistics have also been released. In the second quarter of 2015:
- There were 3.175 billion global active Internet users (that is almost half of the world's population!).
- Global penetration of social media is 30%, with more than 2.206 billion active users.
- 1.925 billion mobile users use their mobile device to access social media. platforms.
- Facebook adds half a million new users each day – that is six new profiles per second.
- 12 new active mobile social users are added every day.

Please just consider these numbers. With this many people on social media you have to take SMM seriously. If you ignore SMM, you do so at your peril and the demise of your business. If you ignore SMM, your business *will* be left behind and it *will* fail in today's world.

SMM is also ideal because it is beneficial for any size of business. Back in the old days, prior to the use of the Internet, or even computer technology, only large- and medium-sized businesses that had enough money could really engage in effective marketing. Taking out advertisements in a magazine, on the radio, or on TV would cost literally thousands of dollars, even tens of thousands of dollars. Even for a local business to take out a billboard ad or advertisements in the newspaper would cost hundreds of dollars.

When it comes to SMM, any business can make use of it because it's FREE! All it costs is the time it takes to make the posts, answer questions, and converse and offer something of value to followers and fans. That's it. That's all. Plus, the connection you make with your followers will be far more intimate than you could ever get from a magazine advertisement.

What This Book Offers

If at this point, you are still reading, then you understand the importance of the knowledge contained in this book. SMM is critical to the survival of your business. Like I said above, if you don't get onboard, you *will* be left behind. In the pages that follow, we will go through everything that you need to know about SMM.

The very first thing we will discuss is branding and the importance of branding in marketing and SMM. Knowing how to establish your brand on your social media sites is incredibly important and knowing what makes a good brand will allow you to create a brand that will set you apart from the competition.

Then we will discuss the social media platforms. In this book we will be focusing on the main platforms, which include:

- Facebook
- Twitter
- Instagram
- YouTube
- Pinterest
- LinkedIn

First, we will look at the right types of platforms for your SMM strategy based on your target audience. This means you need to know your audience, how the various platforms work, and the types of people they attract. Then we will devote a chapter to each of the platforms, providing a detailed breakdown of what it is, how to use it, how to connect with your audience, and special features of the platform that will help you in your SMM strategy.

Finally, we will wind up the book by discussing how to make the switch to SMM, including how to get your employees onboard and how to integrate SMM into your current marketing strategy. This discussion is about all things related to posts, pins, widgets, links, embedding, and social media buttons.

So, if you are ready for the social media marketing ride of a lifetime, then strap yourself in because this train is about to take off! Enjoy the ride!

Branding is Everything

"Good content always has an objective; it's created with intent. It therefore carries triggers to action."
Ann Handley

Before you can ever market your business, whether through social media or via any other means, you need to have a brand. Let's think about the traditional use of the word "brand." Branding was a practice originally undertaken by cattle ranchers. They would use a branding iron to mark their cattle before sending them to the slaughterhouse. The brand on the cattle would identify which cattle belonged to which rancher. The brand the rancher used would consist of his initials or a symbol or some combination that related to and identified him as the owner of the cattle.

Skip forward to marketing in our modern consumerist society and branding is still used as a means of identification. In this case, a brand identifies the producer or manufacturer of a product or a line of products. Just think about some of the more common brands that everyone can recognize. Nike has its name, but it also has the Nike swish. All you need to do is see that Nike swish and you know it's a Nike product, whether it's a pair of shoes, a shirt, or a hat.

What about McDonald's? Those golden arches are recognized all over the world. If you are visiting Japan and can't read the language, you will still know where McDonald's is just by looking for those golden arches. The same can be said for Starbucks and it's impossible to miss Coca Cola.

The point is that a brand sticks with consumers. People might not remember the many things a company produces and sells, might not know what new products come out, but if they see that silhouette of an apple with a bite taken out of it on an electronic device, even if they have never seen the device before, they will know it's an Apple product.

What a Brand Is and What It Does for You

What is a brand, specifically? Is it a word? Is it a symbol? A graphic or picture? The answer is all of the above and more. A brand is how a company is recognized and perceived. It is a combination of the company's logo and the way they present themselves. The logo or brand image can include any combination of words, symbols, colors, and images that are brought together to create an esthetically pleasing image or graphic that is recognizable anywhere, at any time.

But branding does more than just provide a way to recognize the origin of a product; it evokes emotion. When someone sees the Starbucks symbol, they might feel relief at finding their favorite coffee. They might feel a sense of warmth and comfort that the coffee house provides on a cold winter evening. The point is that they feel something and you want that something to be positive. How you present yourself on social media will contribute to how people view your brand and whether that view is positive (we'll get into that more later).

"Okay, great," you say. "If branding is such a great way to recognize a product, can I use it if I'm only a small company?" The answer is a resounding yes! Any business, company, organization, or individual can make use of branding and benefit from it. It doesn't matter how big of a company you run. As long as you have a brand, the people who matter will know who you are and what products and services are yours. Regardless of what you want to do online, you want people to know who you are. You want people to recognize you, whether you are selling something, providing information, trying to attract subscribers, or looking for more followers. A brand allows you to accomplish that.

14

Key Rules of a Good Brand in SMM

As simple as many of the brand names you see out there might be, a lot of thought went into each and every one of them. You want your brand to be a good representation of you and your business. You want your brand to be unique, yet simple. You want it to stand out, but not be over-the-top. There are a few key characteristics of a good brand name that you will want to pay close attention to.

Uniqueness
You want your brand to be unique, to stand out from the crowd. If you are an app developer, then you will be competing against all the other app developers out there. You will want to stand out and be noticed among thousands of other app companies. Being unique doesn't just mean having a unique and eye-catching logo; it also means presenting yourself in a unique way. Do you have a special guarantee? Do you set yourself apart by the quality of service you offer?

In other words, you need a unique selling point or a niche that sets you apart from all the other businesses who are selling the same thing that you sell. What can you do that no other business does? Consider it carefully.

Knowledge of the Target Audience
Few businesses target a very wide audience. More likely, your business has a specific target audience and you need to understand who that target audience is when creating your brand. Is your target audience hip 18-30-year-olds or more refined 50-65-year-olds? How you present yourself to these two groups will matter. Are you targeting moms or the businessperson? Again, a different presentation of your business is required, depending on whom you are targeting.

Consistency

This is extremely important. Your brand must represent your business consistently no matter where it appears. You must use the same logo everywhere. Your company bio must be the same everywhere. You must offer the same level of service every time. Your products and services must be of the same quality every time a customer comes back to you. You must maintain a consistent level of responsiveness on social media.

Be Stiff Competition

You need to get your business out there every day. Even if you get some forward momentum, it won't keep going unless you keep active. Your customers cannot keep it going without you. Be innovative. Always find new ways to reach out to your customers, fans, and followers. If you come to a standstill in representing yourself, your business will come to a standstill. It's that simple.

Gain Exposure

Make use of multiple social media platforms to get your business noticed. You will want to have a presence on more than one platform and you must link those platforms together. Link to your Instagram photo on Twitter. Link to your YouTube video on Facebook. Get yourself out there frequently and consistently.

Give Value, Don't Make the Sale

In fact, don't go for the sale at all. When you build a following on social media, your goal is to be – well – social! Social media gives you a unique opportunity to connect with your fans, followers, and customers on a very personal, one-to-one level. You will be able to connect directly with them and you don't want their first impression, or any impression, of you to be that of a pushy sales person. This is all part of building your brand, a brand that, when people think of it, they will think of a kind, helpful, knowledgeable person, rather than just some product or service, or worse, a non-responsive entity that doesn't seem to care or isn't reliable.

When marketing via social media, you are in a unique position to just chat with people. You can answer questions, pose questions, run contests, ask fans to post photos, invite comments, and provide valuable information. In fact, perhaps the most beneficial aspect of SMM is that you can create truly added value for your customers and followers and develop a relationship with each and every one of them. Rather than trying for the direct sale, you can offer your customers something that will enrich their lives in some way, something that is informative and/or uplifting, or something that can make a difference in their lives.

For a moment I want to focus on the relationship aspect of SMM. In the brick-and-mortar world, if you have a store front or an office and you have customers come in, then you can talk with them face-to-face. If they come in more than once, you can begin to develop a relationship with them. But they might not come in every day, and when they do, it's just you and the customer relating to each other.

Now think about how social media works. It's *better* than a store front! No, really. You are not chatting for five minutes with one customer in a completely closed off conversation. You are interacting with multiple customers and followers over the course of hours or days or even weeks and you are involved in conversations between many different people at the same time. You will have a much better opportunity to see what your customers and followers are really like, what they really think, and how you can really make a difference in their lives.

Be an Expert

Another part of building your brand and something that SMM offers is the opportunity to build a reputation as an expert in your field. If you sell pet supplies, being able to weigh in on discussions about different types of pets, the health of animals, the best ways to train a dog, or any other topic that is important to followers and customers is key.

You can answer questions, offer educated opinions, and post links to informational articles you have written. All of these things help build you up as someone who knows what they are talking about, and if you are that knowledgeable about how to train a dog, then you must know the right type of collar. People will be more likely to shop and purchase what they need from you if they trust you. Again, it's all about providing real value for your customers and followers. We'll discuss more of the how-to of providing value and building trust and a reputation later on when discussing each individual platform.

The Logo

I want to focus on the logo here for just a moment. A logo is the graphic or image used to represent your company or your brand. First of all, if you don't have a logo, you need one. It's that simple and it's especially important when engaging in SMM. The logo is all-important because it is the visual means by which your company is recognized everywhere online. Your goal with a logo is to ensure that people will automatically recognize your presence as soon as they see it.

It is a good idea to have a graphic designer to create a logo for you, if you have the means. If you cannot afford a graphic designer or are creative and artistic and want to give it a go on your own, then, there are a few key rules you should follow.

KISS It

Keep It Simple Stupid. Logos do not need to be overly fancy or extravagant. In fact, they shouldn't be. You want to capture the essence of your company and what it has to offer with as simple a presentation as possible. This means minimizing the number of colors, fonts, shapes, images, and lines you use while still presenting yourself in a memorable way.

Plan Ahead

One of the most important parts of creating a killer logo is to plan ahead. Get out a pencil and paper or use design software and just do some drawings or images. Sketch your ideas on paper or on the screen and play around with them. It is not uncommon for seasoned graphic designers to spend more time in this planning stage than on any other stage of logo design.

Suitability

Your logo should suit your company, what you have to offer, and your target audience. For instance, a recent trend in logos is to have 3D graphics that look bubbly and make use of drop shadows and gradients. This might be fine for a social media side or cloud-type storage targeting a younger crowd, but it won't be a good logo for an online drug company whose target audience is over the age of 50. For example: A formal wear company will want to have a more classic presentation than a new emoji site.

Choose Color Carefully

The use of color in logos and graphics is a complex topic, but there are a few rules that, when followed, will ensure you end up with a good logo to which people can relate. These rules include:

- Make sure the colors used are not too bright or they might be hard on the eyes.

- Combinations of colors should be from the same area of the color wheel, meaning warm with warm and cool with cool.
- Make sure the logo looks good in two colors, black and white, and grayscale.

When designing your logo, experiment with various color combinations. You will want the colors used to be in line with the feel of the brand. If you have to break the rules, there needs to be a good reason for doing so, like incorporating more color when your logo will include a rainbow.

Font Type and Size Considerations

Font type and size are important and it can be more difficult to get this right than it might seem. First and foremost, stay away from the most common font types. They are just too common and the result will look very amateur. The best thing to do is to just experiment with different fonts and sizes until you find one that works. Also, remember these two rules:

- Ideally, stick with one font type and definitely use no more than two.
- The font must still be legible if the logo has to be scaled down.

Size *Is* Important

Here I am talking about the overall size of the logo. A logo will be shown in different sizes, depending on where it is displayed. On your company website, you can devote a large space for your logo, but when it is a thumbnail on a social media site, it still has to be recognizable and legible. You will need to test the logo at various sizes to be sure it looks good at any size and in any medium.

Achieve Balance

Any form of art – yes a logo is a form of art! – requires balance. Balance is the use of space, both white space and colors and graphics. How these are presented or how the graphics and colors are represented on each side of the design matters. The weight of these aspects of the logo design should be equal on both sides of the logo. There shouldn't be too much white space and there shouldn't be an area that has more going on than another area.

Make It Recognizable

The ultimate goal when creating a logo is to make sure it will be easily recognized. You want your logo to automatically call to mind the brand it represents. That means that you need to design a logo that combines all of the above aspects – color, font, size, and balance – with an original design that captures the eye.

Part of being recognizable is that the logo can be recognized from all angles. When you are testing to see if it is a recognizable logo, you can invert it and do a mirror image and see if each of these can still be recognized.

Engage Your Audience

Now that you are on your way to creating a great brand for your business, you need to know how and where you can make that brand work for you. There are many different platforms out there that you can make use of. In this book we will discuss the most popular ones, the ones the most people tend to use on a daily – and even hourly! – basis.

But first I want to take a moment here to discuss engaging your followers. When you attract followers to your social media sites, you will want to do more than simply grow your numbers. It doesn't matter how many followers you have if they aren't doing anything on your site or getting anything from it. In fact, it is critical that you remember that how you interact with your followers is far more important than how many you have.

Once you have your followers all signed up, you need to engage them, which is an easy way to say that you need to get them interacting with each other and with your brand. How you do this will depend on the social media platform you are using, but can include posts, tweets, photos, questions, contests, and more. The more you engage your followers, the more word-of-mouth is going to gain momentum and attract new followers to your site.

With this in mind, let's move on to a chapter-by-chapter discussion of the various platforms, including platform demographics, how to choose the right platforms to reach your target audience, how to get to know your audience, and the various methods of gaining followers, connecting with them, and engaging them.

Facebook

"Engage, Enlighten, Encourage and especially...just be yourself! Social media is a community effort, everyone is an asset."
Susan Cooper

There are so many social media markets out there and not all of them are going to be right for your business. How do you know which ones to use? Is Facebook the best platform through which to connect with customers? Can you tweet your way to a larger following and a larger market share? The key here is that you have to know your audience, not only in terms of what products or services you have to offer, but also in terms of which people use which social media platforms.

Not all social media networks are the same. Some attract a younger audience, some older. Some tend to have a more professional audience. Some have more action in the evenings and some in the day time. Some are more frequented by women and some more by men. In a nutshell, you need to know who your target audience is and where to find them.
As mentioned previously, in this book we will be focusing on the most popular platforms, which include:

- Facebook
- Twitter
- Instagram
- YouTube
- Pinterest
- LinkedIn

Each chapter from here on will discuss each of these platforms, including information on demographics and knowing your audience and the various ways to connect with your followers and add value to their lives. In this chapter we will discuss Facebook.

Demographics

When it comes to age groups, Facebook tends to be more popular among older people, especially since 2011. According to data gathered between 2011 and 2014 and assessed by iStrategyLabs, use of Facebook among users from between the ages of 13 and 24 dropped by nearly 7 million people. There was a 3.4 million user decrease in the 18-24 age category, which is a decrease of 7.5%.

While the younger users dropped off, Facebook gained a lot of older users, with a growth of 32.6% in the 25-34 demographic, a 41.4% growth in the 35-54 demographic, and a whopping 80.4% growth in the 55+ demographic.

Having said the above regarding age groups, more people still use Facebook than any other social media platform at a total of 72% of adult internet users (Pew Research Center). This makes Facebook a go-to when it comes to SMM. It is also important to note that slightly more women (77%) than men (66%) use Facebook. For those tapping into social media for the purpose of marketing, this data reveals that Facebook is a great platform when reaching out to an older audience and a good way to reach out to women.

Growing Your Audience

It is important to keep growing your audience base. You do not want to stagnate. There are a number of effective ways to gain more followers on Facebook.

The Like Button

Make use of your website to draw people to your Facebook page. If they have taken the trouble to visit your website, then there is a high enough level of interest that they are very likely to be interested in your Facebook page. So – make it easy for them to find it! The easiest way to do this is to add a Facebook Like button to your website. The button can be positioned anywhere on your page and it can be placed on any and all website pages you have, including thank you pages.

Use Your Personal Facebook Profile

No doubt you have your own personal Facebook profile. This can be used to promote your professional Facebook page. You can add your business or company as your current employer and ask any employees you have to do the same. You simply need to go into the **About** page of your personal profile and edit the **Work and Education** section. There you can click on **Add a Workplace**, fill in the details, check "**I currently work here**," and set the visibility to **Public**. Don't forget to save your changes.

Include Your Facebook Page Everywhere

Whether you have published a press release, have been a guest blogger, submitted an informative article to a site, or have established your presence in any other way online, be sure to include a link to your Facebook page. You can do this in an author bio or in information about you or the company.

Use Your E-mail Signature

Despite the explosion of social media, e-mails are still sent every day. You send e-mails to family, friends, acquaintances, customers, suppliers, and many other contacts. Hopefully, you already have a professional signature that appears at the bottom of each e-mail. Now be sure to include a link to your Facebook page in that signature. You can also include your Facebook link in your signature on any forums to which you post.

Share via Other Social Media Platforms
If you have followers on other social media platforms, then you can ask them to follow you on Facebook, as well. Include the request in your tweets or posts and keep it casual.

Make Use of Facebook Ads
You can easily promote your Facebook page by creating an ad for it. This allows you to target specific audiences and markets that suit the content of your page. Facebook truly has incredible options for targeting your audience. You can combine different demographic options, such as those who have a salary above $75,000 and own a motorcycle or those who vacation twice a year and own a dog. The combinations are endless.

Interact with Others via Your Page
When you are cruising Facebook and checking out the pages of others in your industry or field, you can do it as your company page, rather than using your personal profile. All you need to do is access your Facebook dashboard and select your professional page instead of your personal profile. Whenever you comment on another Facebook page, your professional page will be seen by others.

Create Groups and Events
Everyone is a member of at least one Facebook group, right? You are, aren't you? Facebook groups can be created by anyone at any time and they are perfect for anyone who wants to promote their brand. Groups allow you to offer extra value to your fans and customers. You can offer them motivation, discuss current events, keep in touch with your biggest fans (who can become your brand ambassadors), promote events, build your community, strengthen your team of employees, and promote company culture.

Events are also an important way to help market your brand via Facebook. If you have a physical business location or plan to hold an event of some sort, create an event page to help promote it and share that event page on your own profile and company Facebook page. Invite everyone you know to your event and share information and the link to the page on other social media accounts and anywhere else you can post a link to the event page. Just remember that when it comes to the event page, make it about the event and not about your business. People will already know about your business or they will find out if they really want to know.

Advertising on Facebook

While we have been talking about creating a Facebook page and building a fan following, it is definitely worth discussing advertising. Yes, you will pay for Facebook's advertising service, but the targeting capabilities of Facebook advertising are worth it. Some of the things you can do with Facebook advertising include:

- Target your current fans.
- Have Facebook target others who have similar Likes and interests as your current fan base.
- Upload your e-mail subscriber list to Facebook and it will target those contacts.
- Target fans of other Facebook pages, including competitors and others in related industries.
- Drive people who visit your website to your blog and then Facebook will track each person that clicks on the blog link.
- Target based on income, age, gender, geographic location, occupation/industry, homeownership status, ethnicity, level of education, or political affiliations/preferences, generation, parental status, and more.

Be sure to use effective graphics in your Facebook ad, and unless you are someone who is very well-known, avoid using your own image and instead focus on the text, making it appealing.

You will have to create a budget for your Facebook ad campaign. Fortunately, it's relatively inexpensive. A good place to start is to spend $5 on each ad set. You will have access to analytics and will be able to determine which ad sets are performing better. You can then focus more advertising dollars on these sets.

Pay close attention to your cost per lead. If it goes above $5, then make changes to your ad to improve it. Change one thing at a time and test it for three days to see if it makes a difference. Start by changing the image, then try changing the text, then something else. If you change all of these at the same time, you won't be able to identify the problem.

Likes Aren't Everything
We have talked at length about how to get more fans on Facebook, but when it comes to Facebook, or any other social media platform, you want more than just likes and followers – you want to engage your audience. You want them to spend time on your page, actively comment on your posts, and get into discussions with you and other fans. There are a number of very effective ways to accomplish this goal.

Photos
According to Marketing Land, readers are four times more likely to be engaged in a Facebook post if it has an image, rather than links. These posts will also get four times the number of shares, two times the number of Likes, and will be 2.5 times more viral. They also found that the use of photos doesn't increase fan growth, but like we discussed above, it's not how many fans you have, but how engaged they are. In this light, photos are the key.

What this means for you is that the more photos you post, the better fan engagement you will get. If possible, post a photo with every update.

Videos

Videos are an incredibly effective marketing tool. We will discuss the profound effect that videos have in the chapter on YouTube, but here it is enough to say that videos are more engaging and totally worth the effort. You can either post a link to your video on YouTube or you can post the video directly on Facebook. Either way, your audience doesn't need to leave Facebook to see the video.

There is an advantage to posting the video directly to Facebook. If you post it as a link, then eventually it will get lost in your ever-growing newsfeed. When it is posted to Facebook, it will always be in the photo album, which means fans can access it easily at any time, and in the process, they will also be able to see any other videos that you have posted.

Questions

To engage your Facebook audience, you want to get them talking. What better way to do that than by posting a question? You can ask questions directly related to your brand or products, but perhaps even better is to ask an indirect question. It is also best to ask open-ended questions. Instead of starting your question with "Do" or "Is," start it with the standard journalistic style "Who," "What," "When," "Where," or "How." You don't want just a yes or no answer; you want to start a conversation between your fans that goes on for a long time. For example, the success coach could ask, "What do you do when you feel rushed for time?" or "What planner or organizer do you use?" The answers will flow in.

Replies to Comments

Whether you have asked a question or made another type of post, you shouldn't just sit and passively observe the responses and comments. Get involved! Your whole goal is to start a conversation and to help people connect with you and your brand. You need to be involved in that conversation. You can respond directly to a specific comment on Facebook and you can make use of this feature to engage in a conversation with your fans.

If the comments do not answer a question, but pose a question about your post, respond to them. It's important to respond to all comments on your Facebook page, even if they are negative. If you avoid the negative comments or delete them, you will lose the trust of your followers. Instead, respond in a positive manner, set the record straight, and make amends if necessary.

Like Comments

If you don't have anything specific to say about someone's comment or response, then the very least you can do is Like the comment or response. This way, you will be showing your fans that you are paying attention to what they are saying and this will go a long way to keeping them engaged.

Encourage People to Post

While people can comment on your posts, you want to encourage them to make their own posts on your Facebook page. This way, your fans can communicate with each other more effectively and the posts will show up on the poster's newsfeed, which means that all of their friends will see it and that will lead them back to your Facebook page.

There are so many ways to get fans posting on your page. Here are a few of them:

- Tell fans they will receive a discount if they post something.

- Ask fans to post a picture of them using your product or a review of your product (offer an incentive).
- Ask fans to post their favorite of, well, anything that is related to your brand – for instance, in the example of the success coach, fans can be asked to give their favorite motivational quote.
- Post in your physical store (if you have one) that you are on social media and invite people to visit your site and post.
- Use Facebook tabs (you can add these to any Facebook page) to allow fans to post a comment or a review, engage in discussions, and more.

Hold Contests
Everyone loves a good contest! Radio contests, free draws, you name it – people love the idea of being able to win something. Running a contest might cost a little extra money, but it will be worth it in the end. There are so many types of contests you can run, such as:

- Sweepstakes
- Photo contest (you can make these photos of your brand or something related to it).
- "Like to Win" – fans can Like a certain post and have a chance to win.
- "Comment to Win" – every fan who comments on a post has a chance to win.
- Photo caption contest – either choose the winner or say the one with the most Likes/comment wins.
- Fill-in-the-Blank contest – the answer can be factual or you can accept funny responses and the winner is the one with the most Likes.

- Q&A contest – ask a question and pick the winner from the correct answers.
- Crowdsourcing contest – asking fans to help choose a new name, logo, or other aspect of your business.

How to Attract Attention to Your Posts

What you post and how you post it is a huge part of the impact you have on Facebook. Previously, we talked about different methods of posting that will effectively capture the attention of your audience, but this section is all about strategy. Yes, there is strategy behind good Facebook posts!

No matter how great your posts are you need to know how to map out your posts for the greatest effect, the best time of day to post, and how to analyze your posts to ensure they are as effective as they can possibly be. Let's take a look at the best strategy for optimizing your Facebook posts.

Plan Ahead
You want to be sure that each and every Facebook post you make meets the needs of your audience. The best way to do that is to map out your posts. If you are a success coach, then you will want to present posts on a wide range of relevant topics, such as:

- Top success tips
- Following your dreams
- Perseverance
- Building good habits
- Ways to improve social skills
- Daily gratification
- Investing in relationships
- Latest news and research

Schedule your posts and create a calendar to which you can refer. Determine which posts will be on which topics and how many posts per week you will use to connect to your blog, your Twitter account, or any other social media accounts that you have. If you can have a content calendar created a week in advance, you are ahead of the game!

Create Skimmable Text

I will discuss this more later on, but I want to touch on it here. The attention span of the average person is decreasing – significantly! In fact, Microsoft recently conducted a study that found the average human attention span is shorter than that of a goldfish! In 2000, at the beginning of our technological revolution, the average attention span for a thought in the human brain was 12 seconds; now it is eight seconds.

You need to keep this in mind when creating your posts, particularly text-based posts. You want them to be easily skimmable by anyone who reads them. Keep them as short as possible, but most importantly, you want to focus on the first three or four words of your post. These are the words that will grab the attention of the reader and keep them reading.

Going back to the example of a success coach, if you are posting about changing habits, consider these two starts to a post:

Learning how to change your habits is critical to your success. (snore)
or
Bad habits you don't know you have. (What bad habits? I don't have any bad habits?)

Readers will skim through the posts. If a post that interests them catches their eye, they will be more inclined to keep reading.

Find the Best Publishing Times

When you post your content is almost as important as how you post your content. When you post will depend on your target audience. In general, it is best to post content on Thursday and Friday and the worst days are Monday to Wednesday. This is because people tend to be tired of work by the end of the week and go on Facebook more throughout the workday on Thursdays and Fridays.

There are also times of the day when there is higher traffic on Facebook. The best time of day to post on Facebook is early afternoon (in the time zone in which the majority of your audience resides). Around 3:00 pm is when you will see the most clicks on your posts. If you can't always post in the afternoon, the general rule is to keep all posts between 9:00 am and 7:00 pm.

Analyze the Content

There really aren't that many formats in which to post on Facebook. You are either going to post text, a link, a video, or an image. What you use is going to depend on your goal with the post. If your post is related to branding, then you will want to stick with videos and images. If you are looking to direct readers to your blog, then you will be posting a link, perhaps in a text post that refers to new research or news related to the post topic. You will use a text post when you pose a question to your readers.

Facebook provides you with Page Insights, which is available to you once at least 30 people Like your page. Through Page Insights you will be able to:

- See your page metrics, the number of Likes, your reach (how many fans are sharing posts or referring your page), and level of audience engagement.

34

- See how viral your posts are and determine this information based on the type of post.
- View the demographics and geographic locations of your Likes.
- Talking About This will let you see who is talking about your page; particularly useful to see trends in content over time.
- Check-in will allow you to see who has been to your physical location, if you have one.

Keeping track of these analytic details will help you hone your Facebook page to increase your readership and spread your content to the masses.

Customization is Key

You can customize your posts even when you post a link. Whenever a link is posted, Facebook automatically grabs all the metadata for the description of that link. Fortunately, you can change this description to suit the needs of your post, making it unique and eye-catching. You can also add keywords distinct to your brand and your post.

Get Started

You are ready to start building a fan base on Facebook. Create your page and start posting. Just remember that the most important thing you can do is offer value through your posts and develop a real relationship with your fans. Once you build a level of trust with them, they will have a natural inclination toward what you have to offer in terms of products and services without feeling pressured. It's a win-win situation for everyone.

Twitter

"Everyone starts out with nobody listening to them and nobody to listen to. How and who you add determines what Twitter will become for you."
Laura Fitton

Twitter is a very different beast than Facebook. While Facebook is the most popular social media platform, Twitter is the least used, although not the least recognizable. Twitter is quicker, less formal, and often less familiar than Facebook. Tweets take moments to create and can reach a huge audience, which makes it a highly effective method of marketing for brands.

Demographics
While Facebook's use is skewed to the older crowd, Twitter tends to be used more by younger people. Overall, Twitter is used less than all the other social media platforms, although it is one of the most recognizable. The Pew Research Center found that 23% of all online people were using Twitter as of the end of 2014. Of those, the highest proportion (32%) of users was in the 18-24 age group. In terms of gender, Pew reported that 25% of males were using Twitter, while 21% of women use it. This is relatively close in terms of balance, but slightly skewed to the male user.

How Twitter Differs from Facebook
In order to increase the amount of engagement on Twitter, you need to understand how Twitter works. You can't use Twitter with the same mindset you have when using Facebook because they are totally different.

Lifespan
Twitter posts, or tweets, have a shorter lifespan than posts on Facebook. The first hour after a tweet is made is the most critical, with 92% of engagement happening during that time. Because tweets have such a short lifespan, tweeting multiple

times per day is not only acceptable, it's preferred. You can have a huge impact posting as much as 1-4 times per hour.

Speed

Since tweets are viewed and passed on so quickly and you can post so many times in one day, it has become a social media platform that allows for the rapid spread of information and messages. When you want someone to know about something that is happening right now, Twitter is the platform to use. You can create content that will go viral in an instant, which makes it perfect for news and important updates.

Interest-based

Twitter is likely to pull together contacts that have similar interests. Of course, Twitter has a serious social component, but what draws people together are common interests. If you are into Taylor Swift, then you'll find other Taylor Swift fans on Twitter. If you're interested in snowboarding, then you'll find contacts with the same interest. People generally interact with each other on a social level within the context of their interests and not so much because they are family, friends, and acquaintances outside of social media. This tends to imply that people don't have as deep a connection with each other on Twitter as they do on Facebook, and while true, it doesn't mean deeper connections can't happen on Twitter.

Increasing Engagement

With the above points in mind, there are very effective ways to engage your followers. This is important, because like Facebook, it's not enough to have loads of followers. You need to engage them and keep them coming back for more in order to develop a relationship with them, even if it is a relationship based on a shared interest. Here are some ways to increase engagement with followers:

Hashtags

Hashtags are the building blocks of Twitter feeds. A hashtag looks like this: #hashtag. People post by using hashtags and you can search topics by using a hashtag. You can use a hashtag to:

- Search for topics of interest
- Connect with the originator of a tweet
- To help people find you and your posts more easily

Twitter Chat

Nearly every industry that has tapped into the power of Twitter uses Twitter Chat. This is a real-time, live Twitter event. You moderate the chat and focus on a single topic of conversation. These chats have the power to really draw together a host and their followers. The chat will have:

- An associated hashtag
- A specified topic/set of questions
- A specific timeframe in which the chat will take place

To host a Twitter chat, there are a number of things you need to consider. First, participate in some chats first to get a feel for what they are like and how they are run. Not only is this helpful when setting up your own chat, but it also allows you to get involved in the greater community of shared interests. Once you have a good feel for chats, choose a topic that is sure to get your followers really interested and intrigued, create a unique and eye-catching hashtag to go with it, and choose the date and time of the Twitter chat. When doing this, you should be sure you know what you hope to accomplish from the chat, whether it's to:

- Gain more followers
- Connect at a deeper level with your current followers

- Expand your reach
- Establish yourself as an authority

You can promote your chat with your regular Twitter followers and put the word out everywhere you can, including on other social media platforms, your website, and via e-mail. Be sure to make everyone feel welcome at the chat and introduce yourself and the topic/first question, but also set the ground rules for participation and any time limits on questions.

A question format is ideal when it comes to engaging participants. Make sure they are open-ended questions starting with "Who," "What," "When," "Where," or "How." During the chat, you can use the Twitter search tool to filter the conversation by hashtag and you can embed the Twitter search widget on your website so people can participate right from there. If your chat starts to trend, meaning it is one of the most active ones at the moment, capture a screen shot and post it on your website and other social media platforms.

When your chat is done, let participants know when the next one will be, if it's scheduled, or create a chat schedule. Follow-up with any new connections you have made and if there were any really great tweets in the chat, embed those in your blog, on your websites, and on other social media platforms. Finally, use a tool such as Hashtags.org to see trending data. You will be able to see how your chat did over a period of time and learn how you might make the next chat better.

Streaming Your Twitter Feed
If you have a Facebook page (and of course you do!) you can stream your Twitter feed right on Facebook via tabs or directly on your timeline. This is a choice you can make based on certain factors. For instance, you might have a small Twitter following but a large Facebook following. By streaming Twitter on your timeline, you will let your Facebook fans know you have a Twitter presence.

If you are going to stream your Twitter content on Facebook, then it needs to be different enough that your Facebook fans have incentive to check out your Twitter feed. This is also a great way to get more content out to your Facebook fans because the ability to put a lot of content out on Facebook is limited. Twitter has more going out more often and if you space things out well, you will reach more followers.

Live Tweeting
Live tweeting is just as it sounds, tweeting as something is happening. You can get real-time content to your followers when they need it the most. This is great for breaking news, conferences, fashion shows, business meetings, and more! As long as what you want to tweet is something worthwhile for your followers, it will be very effective, especially if you add photos to the tweets.

Trends
There are all sorts of trends on Twitter. There are trends that come and go in each industry and there are daily trends that you can find each and every week. Think of #TravelTuesday or #ThrowbackThursday. If you can find a way to share relevant content about these trends on Twitter and link it back to your own Twitter account, then you will attract the attention of new people.

You can also search for top trends on Twitter. Using Twitter search is the easiest way to search. Just go to the official Twitter search page and check out the top trends. The hottest trends will appear on the Twitter homepage and you can also search for trends in specific categories. There are also plenty of third-party apps that will help you identify Twitter trends, such as Twist, Monitter, Hashtags.org.

More about Hashtags

Given their importance, hashtags deserve more attention than the small mention that they were given above. Again, a hashtag looks like this: #hashtag. The importance of the hashtag is probably greater than you might imagine, particularly when it comes to marketing. In 2014, there was an analysis conducted of the world's top 100 brands, and in the last quarter of 2013, 97% of the top 100 brands posted at least one tweet that had a hashtag in it. When it comes to regular tweets, not including replies and retweets, 47% of the companies posted with one hashtag and 67% posted with one or more hashtags.

Since these are the top 100 brands, they must know what they are doing. What that means for you is that you need to get on the hashtag bandwagon. What follows is five simple and smart ways to used hashtags to your advantage when marketing on Twitter.

Combine Hashtags with a Link

There really isn't much to say about this except to give you the statistics. Simply put, tweets with hashtags had 12% more engagement than tweets without hashtags. Plus, the highest engagement of all came from tweets that included a hashtag and a link (more about links below). When your goal is to increase the engagement of your followers, this is really a no-brainer. Add hashtags to your tweets!

Test Your Hashtags

Not all hashtags are equal. You need to know which ones are the most effective and the only way to do that is to test them. When you have something exciting to tweet about, be it a new product, an event, a special news item, some new research, or something else, you can try out a number of different hashtags. The White House did this after their last State of the Union address. They used 26 hashtags the first day and only used the most popular seven of those the following day because they were the hashtags that appealed the most to their audience.

When coming up with your hashtags be creative and use as many as you like. You can weed out the ones that don't get a good response and keep using the ones that do. The higher the follower engagement, the better the hashtag. It's that simple.

Use Hashtags across Multiple Channels
Hashtags have become far more than a simple Twitter handle; they have become the most recognizable identifier across all forms of social media and other forms of media. Take the 48th Super Bowl. Advertisers used hashtags in their Super Bowl ads far more than any other social media identifier. The beauty of the hashtag is that it can be used anywhere, at any time, and it is instantly recognizable.

Mold a Hashtag into a Story
Bring a hashtag alive with more than just the hashtag itself and maybe a bit of information attached to it. Remember, you want engagement. Bind your hashtag to a story, whether it is something about you and your company or about something related. Tell people why you did what you did. Tell them about your company's first success and celebrate it with a contest or a sweepstakes. Tell them anything that is relevant and will get them checking out the hashtag, retweeting, and getting involved.

Not only will this bring about interest in the tweet, it will provide you with a list of new people who have now engaged with your brand. You will be adding followers like crazy with this type of approach.

Track Your Results
You will want to know how well your hashtags are doing when it comes to engagement and response. This is critical. It doesn't do you any good to throw up a few hashtags and just hope they

go viral. You won't know what they are doing if you don't track them, and if you don't know what they are doing, you can't make changes to a hashtag campaign.

When you analyze your hashtags, you can find out a lot of information about their performance. You can also analyze the hashtags of others, including your competition and other niches in your industry. You can find out a lot of information when analyzing your hashtags or the hashtags of others, including:

- Industry influencers
- Demographics
- How many people are using the hashtag
- Competitor comparison
- Industry trends
- Hashtag trends

You can also keep track of ongoing conversations and get involved when you feel the need. And you can get feedback from those who are engaging with your hashtags and get some great crowdsourcing ideas.

There are some great third-party hashtag analyzers out there, such as Locowise, Hashtracking, Tweetchat, and Hashtagify. Using any one of these will allow you to gather important intel on your hashtags, such as:

- An overview of the hashtag's performance
- Top tweets
- An analysis of gender response
- Ranking information
- A timeline of recent messages

Keywords Critical

Keywords are an important part of your Twitter marketing efforts. There are millions of people tweeting at any given time and it would be fabulous if you could connect with them. When you make use of keywords related to your industry, you can connect with them! You can use keywords strategically to reach your target audience based on words that they have used in their own tweets. It's almost like they are drawing a huge, flashing arrow pointing straight at them.

There are two ways to use keywords in your Twitter marketing campaigns. Whenever you use keywords, they will be relevant to both avenues of keyword use, so keep in mind that if you would rather focus on one over the other, then choose your keywords accordingly. Let's take a look.

Search Engine Keywords

People are searching for things all the time on Twitter. They could be looking for the latest music releases, the best vacation hotspots, or the latest toys for their pet cat. Either way, they will be typing in search terms and it is these keywords or phrases you want to tap into. If you can use keyword targeting to target your tweets, then those tweets will appear in the search engine listing that comes up. Essentially, it works a lot like Google search, except it will be your relevant tweets that will show up, rather than your website.

An example of this is if you offer a new type of luggage that is cutting edge. Perhaps it has a solar panel and offers a charging port for your iPhone. You might use keywords in your tweets such as *vacation, luggage, iPhone chargers, top vacation destinations*, and *winter getaways*. Any time anyone searches one of these keywords, your tweet will show up.

Timeline Keywords

When a person tweets something, they are expressing whatever is going on in their life at the moment. These tweets include feelings, thoughts, experiences, needs, and desires and you can take advantage of these tweets. If your keywords match any of the words in someone's tweets, you can reach out to that person. Using the above example, you could reach out to anyone who has tweeted about needing new luggage for that big trip that they just booked simply by targeting keywords such as *new luggage, new suitcase,* or *bigger suitcase.*

How to Attract Attention to Your Tweets
Like marketing on Facebook, you need to plan ahead and have a Twitter marketing strategy in order to attract attention to your tweets. You don't want to simply go into it blind and hope whatever you tweet is going to make a splash. Here are a couple of tips to help you strategize effectively.

Plan Ahead
Planning your tweets ahead will help you plan out a Twitter campaign and take advantage of the time of year, particularly if there is a special holiday around the corner. You will want to start coming up with ideas for your campaign two to three weeks ahead of when you want to tweet. This way you will have time to work holidays and special events into your campaign content and ensure that what you tweet will reach the highest number of people possible.

Planning ahead also entails creating a tweeting schedule. That way you will know when you are tweeting, what you are tweeting, and when you want to link those tweets to other social media posts. This will entail creating an overall SMM content strategy that will involve all of your social media accounts and how Twitter fits in. For instance, if you have a new blog post, schedule out the days that you want to tweet the link to that post. Once isn't good enough! But you have to plan it strategically.

Find the Best Publishing Times

Twitter has different times of day than Facebook that are best for tweeting. In fact, it has different times of day depending on the tweeting you're doing. If you are tweeting B2B (business-to-business), then you will get 14% more engagement on weekdays as opposed to weekends. If you are tweeting B2C (business-to-customer), then you are better off tweeting on Wednesdays and weekends, when engagement is 17% higher.

As for the best times to tweet, the number of retweets will be the highest if you tweet at 5:00 pm. It is possible that people are keeping themselves busy as they head home from work on the subway, bus, or commuter train. The highest CTR will occur between noon and 6:00 pm.

Be Conversational

You don't want to tweet this:
Winter vacationers should check this out...
Instead, you want to invite conversation, like this:
Any winter vacationers out there?
Or:
Where do you like to travel in the winter?

The point is that your tweets should not just let your followers know some sort of information, links, or inspirational quotes, but should present it in such a way as to invite them to respond and start a dialogue with you and with other followers who participate in the discussion.

Aside from asking questions, one great way to accomplish this is to tweet replies to other people's tweets. You can thank someone for their kind remarks or informative response, you can respond to someone's thoughtful reply, and you can further develop the information someone has provided. Here are some tips to keep things conversational:

- Tweet questions

- Ensure a minimum of 30% of your tweets are replies to other people
- Add some of your own insight when tweeting a link to invite conversation on the topic
- Always tweet to your audience, rather than just generic tweets that seem official and way too stuffy

Set Goals

You need to know what you are trying to accomplish by marketing on Twitter. If you don't know what your goals are, then how can you know if what you are doing on Twitter is successful. In fact, 41% of all companies that use Twitter do not know whether or not their efforts are successful. How can anyone run a business like that?

Your goals can be similar to these:

- Build a following on Twitter
- Generate leads
- Bring in more traffic to your website
- Keep track of the reputation of your brand and help improve it
- Have a quick method of responding to customer complaints and concerns
- Network with people of influence in your industry

Your markers for success for these goals will vary and may not be the same as someone else's, but set some markers! You might want to ensure your response rate is over 90%. You might want to keep your response time under 10 minutes. You might want to generate a minimum of 30 leads or get a minimum of 80 new contacts. The point is that your goals need to be specific. They need numbers associated with them. Then you can break them into milestones and you can gauge your success.

Get Started

If you have followed all of the advice written above (I know there's a lot of it), you will be well on your way to a huge Twitter following. As long as you can bring in the followers and keep them engaged, you will be well on your way to a supreme marketing advantage on Twitter. But now that you have seen how Twitter and Facebook work, don't think that is the end of it. There's more! Next we'll check out Instagram, where you can photograph your way to SMM success!

Instagram

"Successful companies in social media function more like entertainment companies, publishers, or party planners than as traditional advertisers."
Erik Qualman

Instagram is all about the saying "a picture's worth a thousand words." All that happens on Instagram is that people share photos and images, yet the effect is powerful. While you'll see the demographics of Instagram in a moment, the most important thing for you to know right now is that despite the fact that Instagram might have fewer active users than Facebook, Twitter, and other social media platforms, it has the highest level of engagement than any other platform.

Forrester conducted a study of 3 million user interactions with over 2,500 brands posting on seven social networks. They found that overall, people do not tend to engage with branded social content. However, Instagram blew the others away providing brands with 58 times the level of engagement per follower than on Facebook and 100 times more engagement per follower than on Twitter. Add that to the fact that Instagram is the fastest growing social media platform among teens and young adults and you have a winning combination.

Demographics

According to the Pew Research Center by September of 2014, 28% of online adults were using Instagram, but of those who use it 55% were in the 18-24 age range, making Instagram highly popular among young adults. It is also interesting to note that Instagram is the only social media platform that is strongly skewed toward an African-American and Hispanic demographic with 47% of users being African-American and 38% of users being Hispanic. Finally, women are more likely to use Instagram at 31% vs. 24% of men.

Increasing Your Following

Your Instagram followers are like gold and it goes without saying that you want as many as possible. Think about it. Every time a follower Likes one of your posts, that post appears on that follower's feed. That means that everyone who is following your follower will see your post and can view your posts, which can further increase your number of followers. There are a number of ways to effectively increase the number of followers you have. Let's take a look.

Hashtags

Yes, hashtags are relevant for Instagram, just as they are for Twitter! And they are formatted the same way – #hashtag. The use of hashtags will help users find your photos because the hashtags will ensure that your photo is grouped with other photos that use the same hashtag. Whenever a user is looking for something in particular, they can simply enter the term into the search box and a list will come up which includes the various hashtags associated with that word. Those using an app on a mobile phone will either use the search function or the Explore button.

Using hashtags is a great way to get your brand out there. You can create a hashtag that is unique to your business, either using your company name or a unique identifier that is easily associated with your brand. For example, if you sell knitted products, your business might be called Knitwits. This would make a great hashtag – #knitwits.

Keep an eye on hashtags that are trending. Anytime a hashtag that is related to your business or industry has gone viral, you can use it in a post and you will ride the viral wave of that hashtag and be visible to more users. The catch here is that Instagram does not actually show what is trending at any given time, but it's a safe bet that whatever is trending on Facebook and Twitter is also trending on Instagram.

You can also use hashtags to connect with niches that are related to your business. This requires some work on your part, but it is well worth the effort. Take the knitting business as an example. Niches might be yarn, baby clothes, socks, scarves, or anything related to a specific type of knitting.

Just remember that when you use hashtags in your Instagram posts, don't overdo it or you might overwhelm and confuse users. Just keep it simple and make sure that you use the most strategic hashtags for your post.

Link to other Social Media Channels
As mentioned previously, linking your various social media channels is critical to increasing awareness of your brand, your social media presence, and your followers. Instagram actually provides the ability to link directly with six other social media networks, including:

- Facebook
- Twitter
- Flickr
- Tumblr
- Mixi
- Foursquare

When you can link to your Facebook and Twitter accounts, you can push your Instagram content directly to those accounts, which saves you time. Any post that is linked to another social media account will show as having come from Instagram, which is a perfect way to let your followers on your other accounts know that you are also on Instagram.

To use the linking ability of Instagram, when uploading your photo, you simply choose the photo and it automatically gives you the option to choose to which other social media platforms you want to post. Just tap on the networks you want (you'll have to log in the first time you do it).

Get Your Website Involved

Instagram makes it super easy to embed your Instagram content on your website or your blog. This is especially effective if your website gets a lot of traffic. You can embed your Instagram feed right in your homepage or portfolio page or you can embed photos and videos in your blog posts. All you need to do is find the photo or video that you want to embed and click on the three dots in the lower right corner. From there you will see the code for the image. You just have to copy and paste the code right into the text file of your blog post and voila!

Likes and Comments

You can use Likes and comments to increase your Twitter following. It takes a little time, but it can garner impressive results. Every time you Like someone's post, that user will see that you did and then they might check out your profile and follow you. You can find relevant images and posts by doing a search of a specific hashtag. Type in the hashtag you wish to search, display it as a list, and go through and Like each associated photo. You can only Like 350 photos per hour, but it is easy enough to do for each hashtag that is relevant to your business.

You can do the same when it comes to commenting on other user's photos. However, there are two things to keep in mind. The first is that you are only allowed to comment on 50 photos per hour and it is a more time-consuming task. The second and most important point is that you need to comment authentically. No sales pitches. Provide positive and honest feedback on the photo and information that is of value if you have it to share.

Engaging Your Audience

The beauty of Instagram lies in its simplicity. There is no sensory overload; there is just an image and a short caption. That's it. But you don't just want your followers to see what you post; you want them to react, engage, show how much they like it, and even get involved with it on a deeper level.

Why is engagement so important? Through engagement, you can see who is interacting with your post. Engagement on Instagram can come in the form of Likes and/or comments and both are important. To accomplish this, there are a number of tactics you can use.

Variety is the Spice of Instagram

Posting the same type of content all the time is *boring*! You need to spice things up a bit. You can rotate between product photos, employees, sneak peaks of new products, events, clients (with their permission, of course!), blog posts, and anything else you can think of. If you have a good variety of content, then your followers will always be excited to check out your latest posts.

Be Authentic

Don't be a sales person. This should go without saying, but it still needs to be said. Just as with Facebook and Twitter, you are on Instagram to socialize with your followers, get to know them, and give them some value through your interactions. Building this kind of relationship and ensuring that your followers trust you can only be accomplished if you are your true and authentic self. If you are anything else, your followers will see right through you.

Know Your Community

You can't build a relationship with someone you don't know. Make sure you are well acquainted with your community. This includes your community of followers and the community formed by those in your industry. Before you even start your own Instagram marketing campaign, you should be on Instagram strictly as a user, checking out what everyone is up to and engaging with users. Getting to know them will help you engage them later on.

Vary Caption Length
While Instagram is about the visual image, captions are often very useful in your posts. Often times you will just post a few words, but Instagram allows up to 2,000 characters, so if you have more to say, and what you can add in text will help capture the attention of your audience and further the emotional experience they have when looking at your photo, then do it! Not all captions need to be just a few words in length. You can play around with different caption lengths and see whether your audience responds better to longer or shorter captions.

Use the Filters
You want your Instagram photos to stand out and give a certain impression. You want them to really attract the attention of your audience. Instagram filters are designed to present your photo with a certain look and feel. You can use these to your advantage. The filters are:

- Normal
- 1977
- Amaro
- Brannan
- Earlybird
- Hefe
- Hudson
- Inkwell
- Kelvin
- Lo-Fi
- Mayfair
- Nashville
- Rise
- Sierra
- Sutro
- Toaster
- Valencia
- Walden
- Willow
- X-Pro II
- Slumber
- Cream
- Ludwig
- Aden
- Perpetua

Of these, the most used include Normal, Earlybird, X-Pro II, Valencia, Rise, Hefe, Amaro, Hudson, Brannan, and Nashville. If you are going for the nostalgic feel, you can use Earlybird or 1977. If you are going for the artsy look, then Rise or Brannan might be more appropriate.

The key is to capture precisely the feel that you want from the photo so that you will invoke the desired emotion in the audience. This will increase engagement. Play around with the various filters to find what works best with the photo that you are posting. Over time, you will become accustomed to the filters and selecting the right one will be a breeze.

Get Involved

If you want other users to engage with your content, one of the best ways to accomplish this is for you to engage with their content. This really pairs with the Likes and comments section above. The whole point of social media is to interact with people on a personal level and develop relationships. This will result in people liking you, as a person, rather than just liking your brand.

Getting involved means actively searching out other users who are in some way related to your brand or your industry. Search for hashtags that are relevant to your industry. If you are an artist, then search out other artists and other forms of art, such as #ArtHistory or #Artist or #ModernArt. When you find interesting content that you truly like, take the time to engage on a personal level. This is about more than just increasing your following; it's about making real connections with like-minded people.

Contents and Campaigns are Key

There are so many ways that you can get followers and users to engage with your brand through contests and campaigns.

These will get followers excited about what you have to offer and get them talking about you. Word of mouth spreads faster when your current followers are engaged with your brand. Here are some contests and campaigns that you can try.

Enter to Win

Essentially, you choose what the prize is that you will give away and then you choose how people will enter. Followers and users will have to do one of the following to be entered into the drawing to win the prize:

- Follow to win (this will increase your number of followers).
- Like to win (like the photo you have posted).
- Submit to win (ask followers and users to follow a URL link and fill out an entry form; this will generate leads).

Once you have all of the details of the contest ironed out, create a post to announce it. Be specific on the dates that the entries will be accepted and once the contest is closed then you can choose your winner at random. Then do a post to announce the winner!

Photo Contest

Having a photo contest is essentially an enter-to-win type of contest, but it's more involved. You will be asking participants to post a specific type of photo. Examples include a photo of their favorite product of yours or of them using one of your products (perhaps the most imaginative way to use a specific product).

Once you decide what you want them to post, you need to be very specific when alerting followers of the contest. Create a unique hashtag that will be associated with the contest and tell followers to tag your Instagram account so their followers can also enter the contest. You can offer those who enter a chance to be featured on your account and on your website or you can offer a prize, but offer something to motivate people to post. This type of contest will really get people engaged.

Influencer Campaign

Influencers are the people on Instagram that have huge followings or have celebrity status. If you can get these users working to help you, then you will reap the benefits. Your focus is on regular users with large followings (celebrities are very difficult to get onboard). Search hashtags relevant to your industry and focus on users that have a minimum of 25,000 followers.

When you find someone you would like to be an influencer for your brand, you will need to get in touch with them and ask. You can do this in one of two ways:

- Direct message the user (you can do this if you follow them) and ask them to help promote your brand.
- E-mail them using the contact information provided (most people provide an e-mail address) and ask for their help.

Be sure to do your homework. You don't only want a user that has a lot of Likes; you also want a user who has a lot of engagement from their followers. Check out at least 30-40 posts to determine what level of engagement the user gets from their followers. You are looking for a lot of followers *and* a lot of Likes/comments.

Video Marketing

Even though Instagram is about photos, you can post videos, too. Videos are a very powerful marketing tool and Instagram allows you to post short videos of up to 15 seconds in length. You can also add filters to your videos.

Videos give you the opportunity to showcase your business and your products in a way no other method can. While we will discuss this in greater detail in the next chapter on YouTube, it is important to point out the basics of what video can accomplish.

Video can help you to create a more intimate connection with your followers. It also gives you the opportunity to give a small demonstration of one of your products, go behind the scenes of your business, or show how something is done. There really is no limit to what you can do. You can also:

- Use user-generated content
- Promote your products (don't go for a hard sale; be creative and subtle)
- Give a sneak peak of something new
- Entertain your followers
- Show yourself doing something incredible

Here are a few tips to follow when creating videos:

- The image is more important than the sound (you can choose to turn on the sound, but it's not the default)
- Make an immediate impact
- Design your video specifically for Instagram, rather than using something generated for another medium
- Make use of the endless loops to make your video start over as soon as it ends
- Be sure to take advantage of special events by capturing them for your followers

How to Attract Attention to Your Posts

As with Facebook and Twitter, you need to be organized in how you approach your Instagram marketing campaign. Posting here and there with no plan will not make the most effective use of the power of Instagram. Instead, you need a strategy that includes a plan of what to post, when to post it, and how to be sure your posts are reaching your audience and achieving the goal of engaging them.

Set Goals
What are you hoping to achieve with your Instagram posts? If you have something to strive for, then you are more likely to post content that will help you meet those goals. You are not on Instagram to sell more products – okay you are, but you won't achieve that unless you go about it indirectly. So you need to set goals that will ensure you reach out to and engage more people. Goals can include:

- Increasing the number of followers by 30%
- Increasing follower engagement by 40%
- Increase non-follower engagement by 20%
- Increase brand awareness
- Show followers what your company culture is like
- Introduce your team and attract new talent

Once you have your goals firmly in mind, and on paper, you will have a better idea of what you are going to post.

Plan Ahead
As with the other social media platforms, plan your Instagram posts in advance and make sure that they reflect your goals. The first thing you will need to do is map out the theme of your content. In other words, determine what features of your brand you want to reveal to your audience. You could have content

61

themes based on different products or services, events, behind the scenes at your company, and company culture.

Take products as an example. You could post tutorials about how to use a product or have customers post photos of the most ingenious use they have come up with for one of your products. You could also show your product in a unique setting or in relation to a holiday.

Once you have determined the content themes you want to use, you will need to set-up a schedule of posts. Set your posting schedule on a month-by-month basis and never for any less than two weeks in advance. Leave some flexibility for spontaneity for those times the unexpected happens, but be sure to plan your content well so that you get all of the variety you need as you cover the various themes.

At all times, keep in mind who your audience is and the overall message that you are trying to send out. You never want to lose sight of your goals.

Post at the Right Time
Instagram engagement over the week is fairly consistent. There is a slight increase in engagement on Mondays and a slight decrease on Sundays, which might influence when you post. As for time of day, it is best to post during off-work hours because engagement is substantially higher during this time.

Analysis is Key
As with Facebook and Twitter, an Instagram campaign isn't really going to do you much good if you don't know how well it is performing. Fortunately, there are many tools out there that can help you in analyzing the performance of each post you make. Perhaps the most popular of these tools is Iconosquare, which is a desktop app that provides a thorough analysis of your posts, including:

- Total number of Likes
- History of the most Liked photos
- Average number of Likes and comments per photo
- Follower growth charts
- Best posting times
- Which followers are the most engaged
- Identification of new and lost followers

Iconosquare also provides users with the ability to add a custom Instagram tab to their Facebook page and to embed your Instagram photo gallery on your website.

Other popular analysis tools include: SimplyMeasured, InstaFollow, Union Metrics, Crowdfire, Curalate, and BlitzMetrics. With the proper analytical tools, you can test out various caption lengths, filters, types of posts, and more to determine which ones generate the most engagement from your followers and other users. This will help you to refine your marketing campaign to make it as effective as possible.

Getting Started

To get started with Instagram, you will need a profile that attracts attention and makes people want to follow you. Creating your profile is the first step in gathering followers. You should add the following to your profile to attract users' attention:

- A great profile photo, preferably of you; people would rather see a person than a store front or business logo.
- A website URL that users can visit.
- An e-mail address that users can use to contact you outside of Instagram.

- A great bio that is unique and will attract attention and that includes your name or your business name and what you do; make sure it's interesting and use keywords that will ensure that you show up on searches relevant to your industry.

A winning presence on Instagram will ensure that your business has the visual appeal it needs to compete in the world of SMM. But there is another way to have a visual presence on social media that works well in conjunction with Instagram – YouTube! Let's take a look.

YouTube

"Content-based marketing gets repeated in social media and increases word-of-mouth mentions; it's the best way to gather buzz about a product."
Marsha Collier

YouTube is a different beast entirely. It can add so much personality and pizzazz to your SMM campaign. What's so special about it? The medium of communication and connection is video and there is so much video can do that other media simply cannot.

First of all, when you post a video of yourself, as opposed to a photograph, people can see the real you. You can actually talk to your audience, interacting with them in a more intimate way. This intimacy is what makes video such a powerful marketing medium.

Demographics

You can think of the use of YouTube for marketing as traditional television advertising meets social media. When it comes to the 18-34 demographic, close to half of these people visited YouTube between December 2013 and February 2014 to watch content. Millennials rated YouTube the best place to watch content. This means that YouTube is a particularly powerful marketing vehicle that you can use to reach out to the younger demographic.

Setting Up Your YouTube Channel

YouTube is no longer simply video-based. They have come up with a new layout called One Channel, which was designed with branding in mind. One Channel allows all of your content to be available and consistent regardless of the screen on which it is viewed. Essentially, you are offering a full-channel experience that will attract subscribers. This is critical to your success when marketing on YouTube.

In order to maximize the benefits of One Channel, you will need to set-up your channel. To do this, you will need to do the following:

- Set your channel icon: This can be a photo or an image (800 px by 800 px), such as your logo, or even a still image from one of your videos.
- Set your channel art: This is what visitors see when they visit your channel. It represents your brand and will act to identify it. The image should be 2560 px by 1440 px.
- Set your trailer: This is a short video that non-subscribers will see. You should think of this trailer as a sort of advertisement for your YouTube channel.
- Add links: You can add one custom link and as many as four links to social media accounts.
- Organize videos and playlists: You will want to keep your audience in mind when you design your programming and One Channel allows you to organize your videos and playlist into sections that you can customize. You can control what your subscribers see and can curate your content into relevant sections.
- Modules: Go into Modules and ensure that every option is checked off so that you can reach out to the greatest possible number of viewers.

Keep in mind as you create your profile that you are promoting your brand. It should be evident in the images you choose (i.e., logo), the color scheme and theme you use, and how you present yourself in every possible way. If you have more than one channel, each one should have an appropriate name and should be under the umbrella of a single company or brand. If you only have one channel, then be sure to brand that channel with a full and proper name.

Engaging Your Audience

The first thing you need to know about marketing via YouTube is that in each of your videos you are not creating an advertisement. As with all other social media channels, your goal is to connect with your audience on a personal level and provide value. If your viewers can begin to trust you as an authority, enjoy your content, and feel as though they know you, then you have done your job well.

Does this mean that you can't have a call-to-action? No. But it does mean that if you are going for the hard sell, you might not find your marketing campaign is all that effective. Instead, you want to provide your viewers with something of value, something they can take away with them, something that they can later say, "Hey, I learned something," or "That was really entertaining." You get the idea.

The honest truth about marketing with YouTube is that you are going to have to learn how to actually produce a video. The more engaged you want your audience, the more video production skills you require. Having said that, it doesn't mean you need to go back to school to get a diploma, but you will need to have a pretty good understand of the following:

- How to tell a story
- Video editing
- Video composition
- Networking
- Search engine optimization (SEO)

Aside from ensuring you have decent equipment with which to film your videos, let's discuss the aspects of video production listed above and a few other things that you need to consider in order to ensure that your audience is engaged.

Story Telling

No matter what content you want to feature in your videos, you want to hook the viewer and keep them watching. The viewer decides in the first 15 seconds whether or not to keep watching, so you had better hook them right away or you'll lose them. Whether you are demonstrating a new product, taking the viewer behind the scenes at your business, doing a how-to, or providing them with a peek at a special event, you need to keep them interested and engaged from start to finish. In short, you can't be boring. Be the life of the video party and bring that party to life immediately! You can hook your audience in the following ways:

- Use a quick, lively introduction that automatically gains the viewer's trust
- Start out with a short clip of what the video will feature
- Tap into your personality and that of any hosts to give teasers for the video and ignite the curiosity of the viewer

Whenever you create a video, you are bringing the audience into your world! Show them your world in the way that you want them to see it. Do you need to be a great storyteller? No. But you do need to be able to evoke emotion from your viewer. The beauty of video is that your audience can hear every inflection in your voice and see every expression on your face, every gesture you make with your body. You can use humor, wit, suspense, and more to create a viewing atmosphere that requires the viewer to keep watching to see what happens.

Video Editing

This is the part that all true artists hate – when they have to start cutting. When you have a raw video, you will find that there are parts that don't really add to the message that you are trying to get across to your viewers, no matter how brilliant it might be. Those parts need to go.

Video editing takes place both before and after production. Before you ever even touch the camera, you should plan out your entire production. Write a script, determine where you will stand, what you will do, and what camera angles you will use. Then you will take what you have planned out and cut anything that does not contribute to the overall message and/or effect of your video.

Once you are done with production, you will then go through the video and edit it. This means you will cut out the parts of the video that do not help deliver the desired message or that disrupt the flow of the composition. What you cut will help determine the pace of the video, allowing you to create the effect you want.

Video Composition
This means knowing how your video will flow from start to finish. The ideal situation is to use a storyboard to determine in what order you want to do things and get your thoughts organized. The last thing you want to do is start filming and have to figure it out as you go. A smoothly flowing video will keep your audience engaged.

Be Yourself
It's important to just be yourself. Do not try to come across as something or someone you are not. If you're not a comical person by nature, then don't try to be. If you are very intellectual, then be intellectual, in an entertaining way. The key is to be genuine. People will see a fake or someone who is trying too hard from a mile away.

Call-to-Action (CTA)

A CTA does not mean that you have to ask someone to buy something. A CTA can be as simple as asking viewers to:

- Subscribe
- Like
- Comment
- Share or Add to Favorites
- Ask viewers to visit your website

If you have done your job well and created a captivating video, your audience will be far more likely to respond to whatever CTA you choose to use.

Optimize Your YouTube Content

SEO

People need to be able to find your videos when they are searching for content. This is where SEO comes into the picture. You need to know what keywords are the best ones to use, you need to optimize your title tag and description, and you need to optimize your video transcript.

First, you need to find the keywords that people are searching the most often. Google Keyword Tool and YouTube Keyword Tool are both ideal for this. Cross-reference the results of both keyword research results to find the top keywords in your industry or niche.

Once you have found your keywords, you need to include them in the title of your video, the description of your video, the video tags, and the video transcript.

Video Title

You video title is the equivalent to the headline of an article. You will want to have your SEO keywords in there, but you also want to word the title so that it grabs the attention of your potential viewers. Try as much as possible to ensure your keywords are closer to the beginning of the title and your branding is closer to the end. If your keywords are Social Media and Online Marketing, then the following are appropriate titles:

See How the Secret to Online Marketing Lies in Your Social Media Accounts

Or

Social Media is the Key to Unlocking Your Online Marketing Strategy

Video Description

You will also use these keywords in your video description. An example of a description using these keywords is:

Breathe life into your **online marketing** campaign using these simple **social media** tricks and increase follower engagement by 20%...

Just be sure that you don't make your video title or description sound like spam – Google doesn't like spam. And be sure to include a link to your call to action within the first two sentences of the description. YouTube automatically truncates video descriptions so that only the first two sentences show and you want your link to be visible without needing the viewer to expand the description.

Video Tags

Video tags are a way for you to tag your video with as many keywords as possible. Choose as many keywords and keyword phrases as you can, placing keyword phrases in quotation marks. The goal is to describe your video in as much detail as possible with the use of short and long-tail keywords.

71

Video Thumbnails

Any YouTube account that is older than 30 days and in good standing gives you the ability to upload custom thumbnails. You can include thumbnails with each video and this can help to attract a greater audience. When you are shooting the video, it is wise to take certain still photos while on location, choosing shots that will make a great thumbnail. Here are some guidelines to follow when choosing thumbnails:

- Close-ups of faces are ideal
- Make sure it looks good at any size
- It must represent the content as accurately as possible
- Ensure the foreground is easily discernable from the background
- Ensure the image is high resolution – at least 640 px by 360 px

Video Annotations

Sometimes, it is useful to have annotations in a video. These are overlays of text that help to explain something, direct the viewer's attention to something in the video, provide additional information, and offer additional ways for the viewer to engage. These annotations should include keywords whenever possible and can include a CTA. You can customize the size, color, and appearance of your annotations. Just be sure of the following:

- Place all annotations in the top two thirds of the video.
- Avoid placing annotations at the very top of the frame.
- Ensure the annotations do not interfere with the audience's view of the video's content.
- Ensure the annotations do not come across as spam.
- Do NOT overuse annotations; too many annotations might distract users from the content of your video and annoy them.

Video Transcript

Finally, you will want to ensure that your keywords are well represented in your video transcript. A transcript is a written record of every word that is spoken in a video, and yes, you should have one. This is an important step and is one reason why planning your video out in advance can help tremendously.

If you write out your script ahead of time, then you will incorporate your keywords appropriately and you will have it at hand to post on YouTube. If not, then you will have to type it out after the video is made. Which do you think is easier? A 1%-2% keyword infusion is good when it comes to your transcript. Just make sure that it sounds natural.

Gaining Subscribers

Subscribers on YouTube are the equivalent of followers on Twitter or Instagram. These are the people who have chosen to keep a close watch on what you post because it is of interest to them. However, even when you have your One Channel set-up and are creating out of this world videos, you will still need to attract subscribers. Do NOT think that just because you posted a few videos, people will flock to your channel and subscribe to it. No, you need to attract people, convince them to subscribe. Here are some ways to accomplish this goal:

Ask

Yes, simply ask for subscribers. This might seem too simple to work, but it does work. You can use a great and persuasive call-to-action and then you can ask viewers to click on the subscribe button. But you need to be specific. People need to be guided when you want them to do something. Tell them exactly what to do and also tell them how they can do it and why they should do it. You can use a line that is something like this at the end of your video:

"To learn more knitting tips and tricks and to learn the stich of the week, subscribe to this YouTube channel. All you have to do is click on the button located above this video."

Use Annotations
We discussed annotations above and they can be used to ask viewers to subscribe to your YouTube channel. You can do this by adding a speech bubble directly below your subscribe button, telling viewers to subscribe to see all your videos. You can also add a Subscribe button right in your video by adding a graphic button to the video and overlaying an annotation on it. Then viewers can just click on the button right in the video.

Use Widgets
If you have a website, blog, or other social media page that gets a lot of traffic, then you can easily add a YouTube widget to the side page to attract more subscribers. All they have to do is click on the widget to subscribe. You can also embed your YouTube videos directly into your blog or on your website.

Make Use of Featured Channels
On YouTube, you can team up with other people who create content. On the main page of your YouTube channel, you will see an option to add "Featured Channels." Choose those who have an audience that is similar to yours and would be attracted to your content and add them to your channel. If those featured channels also add your channel (you simply need to ask them), then you will be able to pick up on many of their followers.

Ensure Consistent Interaction with Viewers
Remember that YouTube is a form of social media. Therefore, you need to be social! Interact with the people who view your videos. If they write a comment, then respond! If any of these people also have videos or a channel, then you can subscribe to their channel and Like and/or comment on their videos. As long as you have something to say and it is genuine, people will respond. Essentially, you have to give a little to get a little.

Motivate People to Subscribe

Give people motivation to subscribe to your channel because one video is often not enough of a reason. If you want to attract more subscribers, then tell people! Offer them a reward as motivation. For instance, you can run a contest. If you get 50 new subscribers over a period of two weeks, then someone will win a prize or you will give something to charity or do something particularly crazy or challenging. The key here is to let people know what your goal is and ask them to support you in reaching it, then give them a motivating reason to do so. This requires little effort and it's fun!

How to Attract Attention to Your Videos

Again, as with any other social media marketing campaign, you need to have a solid strategy in place to make the most of marketing on YouTube. This requires you to plan ahead, post effectively, and make sure you know what is working and what isn't. Let's take a look.

Plan Ahead

Throwing up a random video here and there will not translate into a subscriber base, you need to have a successful marketing campaign on YouTube. You need to have a consistent flow of high-quality videos uploaded to YouTube on a regular basis. To do this, you need to plan an upload schedule and you need to do it well in advance, further in advance than most other social media platforms for the simple reason that you have to leave yourself time to actually produce the videos.

Plan your videos at least a month in advance. This will allow you to take special holidays into account, produce a multi-part series, or follow a theme with your video uploads. Knowing what you will upload and when you will upload it will help ensure that you get the right videos up at the right time and a schedule will also help you to make adjustments when you find that certain videos are performing better than others.

Post at the Right Times

When it comes to posting content on YouTube, there are days and times that work the best to gain the most engagement from viewers and subscribers. The best days of the week overall to post content are Thursday, Friday, and Saturday. This coincides with when people start getting tired of the work week and their focus begins to fade.

As for what time of day is the best for uploading content, that depends. During the weekdays, it is best to upload content in the latter half of the work day. From Mondays to Wednesdays uploading is best done between 2:00 pm and 4:00 pm and Thursdays and Fridays it is best between noon and 3:00 pm. On the weekends, people are more likely to be active on YouTube in the mornings, before they start their errands and weekend activities, so it is best to post content between 9:00 am and 11:00 am.

Conduct a Thorough Analysis

You cannot make changes to your marketing campaign if you don't know what type of response your campaign is receiving. Fortunately, YouTube has its own analytics tool and it will give you a lot of solid information about your audience and how they are reacting to your content. The first area that is significant in terms of YouTube analytics is in regards to viewership. With YouTube analytics, you can see:

- The most viewed days and weeks (while the previous section laid out the best general days and times, you will be able to hone in on what works best for you).
- The most viewed videos.
- What caught people's attention and caused them to view your video (i.e., trending news in your industry).

It is also wise to browse the comments on your videos, not only to interact with your viewers, but to see what they are saying. You might find some useful information from them regarding what attracted them to your videos. Finally, always make sure that the videos that are getting more viewers are annotated to promote your other videos.

YouTube will also make it possible for you to see how long viewers are watching your videos. Are they watching the first 20 seconds or half or the entire video? This is known as watch-time and it is incredibly important, particularly because when it comes to YouTube's search engine, the watch-time of a video affects how high it is ranked in YouTube's search engine. Determine which of your videos have higher watch-times and annotate these videos to promote your other videos.

Finally, you want to know the source of your YouTube traffic. Traffic source is the tool that you can use to discover how viewers were directed to your video, whether they were driven by suggested video placement or related videos. You can even use YouTube's Other Features to view the traffic that you are receiving due to annotations in other videos. All of this information will help you to refine your thumbnails, tags, and metadata. Always analyze the first couple of weeks of your best performers to determine what is driving viewers to those videos.

Getting Started
Now that you have the power of video at your fingertips, you are ready to take your brand to the next level with YouTube. You can do some truly remarkable things and get really creative with YouTube, perhaps more than with any other social media platform. And now that you have an insider's view into Facebook, Twitter, Instagram, and YouTube, it's time to introduce our final two social media platforms, both of which are quite different. Let's start with Pinterest.

Pinterest

"Lead people with what they want. – Lead with what they've already said. – Lead people from where they're at. – Lead them with the things that concern them."
Sandi Karkowski

Once again, much like with YouTube, Pinterest is a different beast when it comes to marketing. Well, sort of... On Pinterest you want to pin things rather than post things, but you still want to get those pins noticed and shared. But first, what is Pinterest? It is social media that is interest-driven, hence its name. People on Pinterest look for projects, instructions, recipes, ways of doing things, and ideas. It is a place to which people go for inspiration and ideas. They are the do-it-yourselfers of the world.

Since Pinterest is interest-driven, it is the ideal platform on which to grow your brand recognition. Let's put this into perspective. In 2014, there was a 27% increase in Fortune 500 companies on Pinterest. Why would successful companies like those be interested in Pinterest if it wasn't worth it? These are not companies that make mistakes and they don't make a move without doing their homework.

Demographics

Pew Research Center reported that as of September 2014, 28% of online adults were using Pinterest, compared to only 21% in August 2013. This is indicative of the growth of Pinterest use. Pinterest is a particularly powerful platform to reach out to women, with 42% of online women using Pinterest, compared to only 13% of men. Having said that, the number of male users grew 5% between 2013 and 2014 and continue to grow, so don't discount them.

Younger people are using Pinterest, with 34% of Pinterest users in 2014 being in the 18-29 demographic. However, use among people above the age of 50 increased dramatically from 2013 to 2014. In addition, more people in the higher income demographics and rural areas tend to be Pinterest users.

Pinterest for Business

Yes, Pinterest offers the option of creating a business account, which is not the same as a personal account. But it is the business account that you will need in order to really have a successful marketing campaign on Pinterest. There are a number of differences between the Pinterest personal and business accounts that you will find incredibly useful.

Terms of Service

You need to make sure that you understand the business terms of service when it comes to Pinterest. The Pin Etiquette Policy and the Acceptable Use Policy are both the same as with a personal account, but there are additional brand guidelines for business accounts. Here are a few of these and a complete list can be found on the Pinterest for business website (https://business.pinterest.com/en/brand-guidelines):

- Do not use the word pin or any phrases that indicate "pinning" to refer to other activities (it is unique to Pinterest).
- Ensure your colors, services, and apps are distinct from those of Pinterest.
- Ensure it is obvious that your pins come from your business, rather than from Pinterest.
- Ensure anytime you use the word Pinterest it is not used alone, but as part of a phrase, such as "Follow us on Pinterest".

- Ensure that it is not implied that Pinterest is endorsing or sponsoring your business; for example, ensure your logo is bigger and more visible that the Pinterest logo.
- You may not run a sweepstake for which entry involves pinning, repining, or liking a pin.

Marketing Education

Pinterest wants you to succeed in your marketing efforts, which is why they don't just provide you with a business account; they also provide you with the education and training to make the most of it. You can enjoy interactive workshops through their Pinstitute and you can enjoy a variety of webinars and other resources that will help small businesses get started.

Analytics

You don't have to look any further than Pinterest itself to find good analytics for your marketing campaign. Pinterest has all the tools that you need to track activity related to your pins.

Rich Pins

You have access to five different types of Rich Pins. Rich Pins offer the viewer more information that a regular pin, which will allow you to improve the sales power of your Pinterest marketing campaign.

Business-oriented Settings

The settings for the Pinterest business account are different than those of a personal account. For instance, rather than requiring a first and last name, you can use your business name. Unfortunately, this means that you will need to manually add your Facebook tab to your homepage on Pinterest.

Build Your Board

On Pinterest you will want to create at least one board for your pins. The board is the way that you organize your pins so that they make sense to viewer. You can consider the board as containing visual bookmarks of the content in your pins. So before you can pin, you need a board.

You can access "Create a Board" from your profile page. Once you click on it, you will see a box in which you will enter the appropriate information, including:

- Board name
- Board description (while optional, this is very important in your marketing efforts because it helps people find your pins more easily)
- Category
- Whether or not you wish to allow others to access your board
- Who can add pins, meaning you can invite other Pinterest users to pin to your board

You can build a board for different aspects of your business. There are several ideas for boards that are useful, including boards for:

- Topics of interest to your target audience
- Educational pins
- Feedback from customers and viewers
- Upcoming events
- New products/services
- Different boards for different product lines
- Company culture and employees
- Provide social proof of your products/services in use (show your customers using your brand)
- Discussion group

How to Make the Best Pins

As with any other social media platform, you want to be sure that your pins can be found by anyone searching for related topics. In other words, your pins should be searchable. There are a number of ways that you can be sure that your pins stand out and get noticed, making your marketing and branding efforts worth the results.

Categories

I know that I mentioned categories briefly in the previous section on building your board, but they are of the utmost importance when it comes to people finding your pins, so they deserve more attention. First of all, when the popularity of categories is analyzed for Pinterest, the analysis is gender-based. Some categories are going to appeal to women more than men and vice versa. Some categories will attract the attention of both. In 2014, a University of Minnesota study of Pinterest determined the top ten categories, as follows:

1. Food & drink
2. DIY & crafts
3. Home décor
4. Women's fashion
5. Other
6. Weddings
7. Design
8. Hair & beauty
9. Art
10. Kids

Most of the first ten categories are favored by women (except art and design), but men still show significant interest in many of them. Other popular categories favored by men include travel, music, sports, technology, cars & motorcycles, and men's fashion.

SEO

Yes, even though Pinterest is a very visual platform, you still need to consider search engine optimization or SEO, which is the use of keywords in the titles of your pins and any text associated with them. We have discussed the use of SEO for other platforms, but here is a brief review. You need to do some keyword research by using a research tool. Once you find the best keywords for your industry or the niche in which you are pinning, you need to work them into your pin titles, descriptions, and file names. Be sure that the titles and text sounds natural.

Images

Pinterest is a visual display of what you have to offer, so it makes sense that the popularity of your pins will hinge largely on the quality and type of images you use. You want all images to be professional and visually appealing (that should go without saying). In order to achieve this, ensure all photos have the following properties:

- High resolution
- Lighter (rather than darker) – lighter images are 20 times more likely to be repinned
- No faces – these are repinned 23% more than photos with faces
- Simplicity – nothing complicated

Pin Size

All pins have the same width of 726 pixels. While the length of a pin is unlimited, the best length to use is 1102 pixels. A pin that is 736 x 1102 pixels will attract the most attention, most of the time...

Use Instructographics

Having said the above about the optimal length for a post, the fact that you can make it any length that you want to has its advantages. If you want to share a how-to, show how to do a craft or decorate a room, or anything else that requires instruction, an instructographic is ideal. Instructographic is a word created by Pinterest and it is a very effective way to connect with followers who are into crafting and DIY.

So what is an instructographic? It is a set of instructions that are laid out step-by-step, but are visual instead of text-based. So instead of the steps being a series of text-based instructions, they are a series of images, diagrams, or photographs that can be followed. Of course, you can include text in your infographics.

Engaging Your Audience

As with all of the other forms of social media we have discussed, you don't want people to just follow your pins, you want them to interact with you and your brand via your pins. How do you accomplish this on Pinterest? There are actually quite a number of ways to engage your audience on Pinterest that are fun and exciting for both your audience and for you.

Competitions

Running a competition on Pinterest is not only easy, it's fun! You can use any pins that are relevant to your brand. If you are a photography company, then you can ask your audience to share their photographs, perhaps using your equipment. Or you can make it a theme. If you are a pet supply company, have people pin photos of their pets using your products.

Whatever you choose to do, make sure that your audience knows that to enter the competition, they need to add your Pinterest site as a contributor to their board. This way, they get shares and new followers and the person with the best photo wins whatever prize you choose.

Allow Board Contributors

You can change any of your followers to being contributors to your board. This will help them to feel more connected to your brand and they will also be advocates for your brand. Maybe your fans will have unique ideas on how to use your products or will want to show them in action in fun situations. For example, if you run a gardening business, you can allow contributors to post photos of their own gardens.

All you have to do to allow your fans to be contributors to your board is go into **Edit Board** and under **Who can pin?** type the name of the fan that you are allowing to contribute. Give your fans the option to contribute their pins to your board and you will be surprised at how it will take off. Your fans will pin and repin more and more and they will essentially do a lot of your work for you, leaving you more time to maintain your social media marketing campaign and run your business.

Offers

You can always run special offers for your fans. You can offer sales, free giveaways, or bonuses. Use the images that you pin to promote your offer. There are two ways to do this. You can pin images from your website and use the description to provide the details of the offer, or you can design an image specifically for Pinterest that includes an offer. Use your imagination and get creative. You want your fans to have to do something in order to unlock a special offer, which might mean pinning and repinning your pin. Once you reach a certain number of pins, your offer will become available.

Understand Your Fans

Everyone who follows you wants something related to your brand so it is important that the images that you pin are directly related to your brand and how it relates to your fans' lifestyles.

This will include images of your products and of those products being used. If you have different boards, then split up your brand into different categories based on those boards and pin relevant images. This will drive engagement and promote your brand as a leader in your industry.

Use Multiple Images

Every web page that you have should have a minimum of one shareable image, which will be a minimum of 110 x 100 pixels. Ideally, you will have more than one of these shareable images on each of your pages. That way, each person who visits your page will have a choice of what to pin and can choose their favorites, something that is of added value to your fans. Remember that if there are no shareable images, your page cannot be shared.

How to Attract Attention to Your Pins

You want your pins to get noticed. That's the whole point of pinning content. It doesn't matter how fabulous and engaging your pins are if no one sees them. There are a few things to consider when attracting attention to your pins, so let's take a look.

Pin at the Right Times

The absolute best day of the week to pin content is on Saturday. The best time of day to pin is 8:00 pm to 11:00 pm, with the peak Pinterest activity occurring at 9:00 pm. Having said this, when it comes to fashion-related pins, the best time to pin is Friday at 3:00 pm.

Pinning from Your Site

Hopefully, you have a website that gets high traffic. You want visitors to your site to be able to easily pin something from your site so they can share it with their followers. Any image you have on your site can have a hovering Pin It button added to it.

You can also add a Pinterest button that allows anyone visiting your website to go straight to your Pinterest site.

Connect Social Media Platforms

You can easily connect your Pinterest business account with your Facebook and Twitter accounts. This will allow your followers on these other social media sites to easily find you on Pinterest, which is ideal because you don't have to start from scratch that way. Plus, you will be able to show your Pinterest content across other social media platforms, gaining more exposure for your pins.

In order to connect to your other social media accounts, you simply go into Settings, click on Social Networks, and connect with the desired accounts. Be aware that this process won't work with Facebook if you have a business page; it only works with a personal Facebook account.

Share via Newsletter

If you send out newsletters, then you can easily include your latest pins, inviting subscribers to visit your Pinterest page and check them out. You can include a line, such as, "Check out our most popular pins this week and visit out Pinterest site for more!"

Plan Your Pins

As with the other forms of social media we have discussed, you shouldn't just randomly pin images. There should be a method to your pinning that revolves around the calendar and special events. Plan out your pins at least two weeks in advance, making sure to take into account any holidays, the seasons, the weather, and anything else that is relevant to your brand. You can also follow a theme with your pins if you plan ahead of time.

Analytics

I mentioned Pinterest Analytics earlier in this chapter. This is a built in tool that is available for Pinterest for business. Pinterest Analytics will help you to determine the following:

- Which of your pins are the most popular
- What people are saving from your website
- Information on your audience, including gender, location, interests, what other businesses they are following, and more
- How much traffic you get to your website as a result of adding a Pin It button
- What types of devices are being used when people are pinning your pins
- Insights on how you can improve impressions, repins, and clicks to refine your marketing strategy and reach more fans

Getting Started

Now you have what it takes to create a fabulous and successful Pinterest site with multiple boards and captivating pins. With the ability to link your web pages to your Pinterest boards, you will increase traffic on all of your pages and increase your visibility. Once your Pinterest boards are set-up, there is nothing to wait for. The quicker you start pinning, the quicker you see results.

LinkedIn

"LinkedIn is a channel to increase, not a tool to replace, your networking efforts, and it is an excellent vehicle to facilitate some facets of your marketing and business strategies."
Viveka vonRosen

LinkedIn is a social media platform that is primarily used by professionals and it is the largest professional social media network in the world. For this reason, this is a particularly powerful form of a business-to-business (B2B) social networking platform that will empower you to reach out to other businesses and brands. While the majority of people who have a profile on LinkedIn use it as a form of resume, there is so much more that can be done with LinkedIn.

LinkedIn is a very powerful marketing tool that can help you to promote yourself and your brand in a way that no other social media platform can. Just remember that in order to be successful marketing your brand via LinkedIn, you need to make a long-term commitment to your marketing plan, just as you would with any other social marketing platform.

Demographics

The Pew Research Center reported that as of September 2014, 28% of online adult internet users used LinkedIn. However, the important thing to note with LinkedIn is that it is particularly popular with professionals, particularly college graduates, employed individuals, and households with higher incomes. The gender split for LinkedIn use is about even, but note that 50% of those with a college education are using LinkedIn and 44% of those with household incomes that exceed $75,000 annually. The majority of users are within the 30-49 and 50-64 age ranges.

Setting Up Your Company Page

Rather than a regular LinkedIn profile, you will want to set-up a company page. Let's go over how to do that.

Company Information

Once you have your account set-up and you are signed in, go to the **Interests** tab at the top of your homepage and choose **Companies**. It will then show you a **Create Company Page** box in which you can click on **Create**. You can then enter your company information, including name and e-mail address. Then click on **Continue** and you can fill in the details of your company. This is where you can talk about your products and services. You don't want this to be lengthy, but you want it to stand out, to describe the value you have to offer in just a couple of sentences.

Logo and Banner

Next, you want to upload your company logo and a banner image. Don't skip this step because people will see your logo long before they will see anything else on your page. It will show up on all staff profiles, so you will want to be sure that every staff member with a LinkedIn profile adds the company page to their profile. When uploading your logo, make sure that you first resize it to 100 x 60 pixels and another one to 50 x 50 pixels. The square is the logo that will appear on the feeds of the followers.

You will also need a banner, something that stands out and delivers a clear message about your brand. If you don't already have a banner designed, there are plenty of design tools you can use to create one. You will want your banner to be 646 x 220 pixels. Think of the banner as being similar to the cover photo on Facebook. It is located on the Home tab of your company page.

The banner can have on it a short phrase that promotes the brand or it can show an image of a customer using a product. It can also show your workplace in a welcoming way. Don't be shy about it. You want this banner to catch the attention of anyone who sees it.

Career and Products

There are sidebars dedicated to your company's products and careers that are located on the home page. This increases the convenience for visitors to your page. You might not need to use the careers section of the home page - that will depend on the type and size of your business. If you don't use it, then the sidebar location will display your company logo with the default text that says, "Learn more about our company and culture."

However, since you have a company, you have some sort of product and/or service and it is important to make use of this section. One important thing to note is that the very first product or service that you feature in the Products and Services section will show up on the **Products and Services** sidebar. For this reason, make this a product or service that really stands out. This should be your primary product or service and you should set it up in a way that it really grabs the attention of your audience.

Remember that when it comes to what you offer, you don't have to stick with traditional products and services. You might have free or promotional offers, free downloads, special reports, podcasts, events, or any number of other things to offer your audience. The more unique the content in the Products and Services area, the more interested your visitors will be in what you have to offer.

Product Recommendations

Your Company Page will have a **Products and Services** tab at the top and when visitors click on this tab, they will be taken to your Product and Services page. One of the best things that you can do on the Products and Services page is feature product recommendations. These aren't the products and services you are recommending; these are the products and services other people are recommending. If any visitor has anyone in their network who recommends your products and services, this is extremely valuable to your visibility and your credibility. How do you get these recommendations? All you need to do is ask. When you go to the page of a specific product, you will see a **Request recommendations** button at the top. Click on that and you will see a drop-down menu. In the **To:** section, you can type in the names of the connections that you want to ask and then click **Send message**. You can even run a campaign during which you ask existing customers and clients to make recommendations. It's that simple.

At the top of the Products and Services page you can also offer a free demo of a product (such as software) or service. This will entice people to try it out and you can include a call-to-action. You can also include a selection of free webinars and eBooks to entice visitors.

Updating Content
This is the critical part of your company page and this is the main feature of your Home page. You want to post content that is related to your company, but relevant to your audience. In other words, you are not trying to do direct sales. Instead, you want to encourage discussion and audience participation. You want to offer industry advice, news, and information. You want to encourage thought leadership through your content.

We will discuss audience engagement further on, but for now it is enough to say that you want to offer something of value to your audience. Tips, tricks, advice, and resources that are industry related make for the perfect content. You can help solve problems or give people ways to make their jobs easier. You can also give tips on time management, stress management, and any other topic that you can relate to your industry and that will be valuable to your audience and you can post events, run polls, and ask questions. The key is to provide content that people will be able to interact with and will be more likely to share with their peers.

There are a few last-minute things to know about updates:

- You can have a featured update that will be visible at the top of your Home page
- Feature posts that have received a good response from your followers
- You can target your audience for each individual update, choosing which followers you wish to see the content
- Review your updates regularly, preferably daily, to see how they are performing (you won't see any statistics in the first 24 hours)

Improving Your Profile's Visibility

Again, as with any of the other social media platforms, having a LinkedIn company page isn't going to do you much good if no one knows it's there. Fortunately, LinkedIn offers a few ways to help increase your Company Page's visibility. When reading through these following ideas please keep in mind that the most successful LinkedIn profiles use a combination of followers, engaging updates, and product/service recommendations to improve visibility.

Employees

Your employees, if you have them, are gold. They are one of the best resources that you have when it comes to promoting your LinkedIn Company Page. Make sure that every employee adds the Company Page to their personal LinkedIn profile. They will get all of the company updates and it will be easy for them to share those updates with their networks.

Use the Link

You can place the link to your Company Page in your e-mail signature, as well as in blogs, article bylines, newsletters, and anywhere else that there is text that is promoting you or your company.

Follow Company Button

LinkedIn has a **Follow Company** button that you can include on any website. Put it on your primary website, on your blog, and on all of the pages of your website. This button makes it easy for anyone visiting your website or blog to follow you on LinkedIn.

Connect with Twitter

You will find the **Twitter** link just above the **Public Profile** link on LinkedIn and this is where you can enter your Twitter handle. Once you do this, every company update you make on LinkedIn will appear in your Twitter feed, tapping into and maximizing your Twitter following.

Customize Your Overview Page

Your Overview page is something that you can really customize and work with to attract more attention to your Company Page. On the Overview page, it will be only the top part of your company description that will be visible. That means that you have to make the first few lines of your description count. You want to do two things in this very important space:

- Give visitors a reason to follow your Company Page.
- Provide a call-to-action that will take visitors to your Products and Services page, where they will find a free demo or a newsletter or free eBook, something that will generate leads.

Networking

Why just sit and wait for other people to engage with you when you can make the first move? If you see a company that you would like to work for, be affiliated with, team up with, or it just shares the same industry as you, make the effort to connect with them on their Company Page. You can respond to the status updates of individuals and companies. If a company posts a resource that is helpful to you and your followers, share it and publicly thank them for it. Like, Share, and comment on updates from other companies. This kind of activity will put you on their radar and your visibility will grow.

LinkedIn Ads

LinkedIn offers the option of using social ads to help build followers and/or product or service recommendations. LinkedIn ads are affordable and are highly effective in increasing the visibility of your LinkedIn profile. Simply run a LinkedIn social ad that asks users to follow you or make a product or service recommendation. These ads can be targeted to specific segments of LinkedIn's membership.

LinkedIn also has the ability to generate direct ads that will target your advertising campaign. This works the same way that Google Ads works. You will create an ad with a headline, some copy, and a link, and you will bid on the amount that you will pay each time someone clicks on your ad.

LinkedIn Apps

LinkedIn also has an Applications area and you can access it and add relevant apps that will help those who visit your Company Page have a better experience. This can include adding blog posts, a list of industry-related books that you are reading, and polls that will help to determine what your followers are thinking.

LinkedIn Answers

This is a highly underused tool on LinkedIn. LinkedIn Answers is a place that anyone who has questions in an industry can go to ask a question and get answers and advice. You can be a person who, as an industry-insider, provides those answers and advice because you are highly knowledgeable in your industry. This will promote you as an expert in your industry and help generate leads and new business.

Engaging Your Audience

Once you have your number of followers growing, you need to keep these followers and keep them active. You do this via your content.

Status Updates

While you want to promote blog posts and exciting company news, these should not form the meat of your status updates. You want to provide updates that are interesting, intriguing, and will engage your followers. Consider status updates that:

- Present controversial news
- Ask a question
- Offer to make a charitable donation for reaching a certain number of followers
- Hold a contest or competition
- Include intriguing and interesting videos or images
- Simply ask your followers to Like or Share your update

A good example of a status update is the following: post a link to a great article on tips or tricks for a specific topic in your industry. You can say what your favorite tips are and then ask your followers/visitors what their favorites are. It gets them reading and engaging in conversation with you and other followers. Remember that engaging your followers means:

- Participating in the conversation
- Producing quality content that adds value for your followers
- Ensuring that you provide variety in your content
- Posting on a consistent and frequent basis
- Not posting with the intent of "making the sale"

Showcase Pages
A showcase page is an extension of your company page that will allow you to focus on certain product lines or services that you have to offer. This allows you to differentiate between your various product lines and target different segments of your audience.

For instance, an outdoor adventure store will offer many different types of product lines. There will be camping gear, climbing gear, ski and snowboard equipment, cycling gear, and more. You can set-up a showcase page for each of these so that the people who are interested in climbing, won't have to wade through the content related to camping and fishing, skiing, or cycling. Having showcase pages targeting different segments of your audience will increase engagement.

LinkedIn Groups
There are two things you need to do here. The first is to join LinkedIn Groups in your industry. Don't just join the obvious ones, the ones inside your industry; also join groups of interest that are outside your industry. This way you will be able to expand your reach to new audiences. As an example, if you are a landscaper, you will want to join landscaping groups, but you can also branch out and join groups in the gardening industry, farming, gardening and landscaping tools, and any other groups that are related to, but not within your immediate circle of influence.

Second, you will want to start your own LinkedIn Group. This is the perfect way to increase visibility and engagement and it will help establish your company as a leader in your industry. You will want to attract members that have common interests and goals and you will want to manage the group well. Take on or assign someone the responsibility of managing the group membership and moderating posts. Get involved and engage with members via making posts and commenting on the posts others make. Be sure your network knows of the group so they can join. These people will include:

- Colleagues
- Industry peers
- Employees
- Clients/customers
- Vendors
- Partners
- Other influencers in your industry

When you have a LinkedIn Group, you can send a direct message each week to all of your members, which goes directly to their inbox. This will inform them of special offers, promotions, and campaigns that you are running.

How to Attract Attention to Your Profile

In order to optimize the amount of attention your Company page and company updates are receiving, you need to understand how and when to attract attention to those updates. This requires planning and the optimization of when you are posting. It also requires you to analyze what is going well and what isn't, so you can adjust your campaign as needed.

Plan Ahead

First things first. If you are going to conduct a LinkedIn marketing campaign, then you need to plan it out. This means that you must first determine what your goals are. Obviously, when implementing a LinkedIn campaign, you will be able to build awareness of your company and brand, generate leads, and establish yourself and your company as a leader in your industry, but what, beyond these things, do you wish to accomplish?

You will need to define the specific metrics that you will use to determine your success with your campaign. You have a number of options:

- Improving the visibility of your brand (increasing impressions)
- Increasing engagement with followers and potential customers (shares, likes, and comments)
- Increasing the external website traffic for your company (increasing clicks)
- Conversion of leads (those who opt-in)

Do you want to do one or more of the above? The key is to determine which of these your goals are and then plan out your company updates accordingly. Your company updates should be mapped out at least two weeks in advance and should focus on the goals you have chosen. If you want to increase engagement, then your company updates will need to support that engagement through posts that ask questions and otherwise encourage followers to comment, share, or like the update. If you want to convert leads, then you will need to include some sort of enticing content and a call-to-action.

The bottom line is don't wing it and don't post randomly. You need to plan your posts around holidays, industry-specific timelines, special events in the industry, industry news, and anything else that is relevant.

Post at the Right Times

Because LinkedIn is primarily used by professionals, users are most likely to be online during business hours. Posts should be made during these times, but Mondays and Fridays receive far less action than midweek. The best days are Tuesday through Thursday. The highest number of clicks and shares are likely to come on Tuesdays between 10:00 am and 11:00 am, which makes this the best time to make your most important post of the week. Other good times to post on peek weekdays are 7:00 am to 8:00 am and 5:00 pm to 6:00 pm.

Conduct a Thorough Analysis

As with any other type of social media, you will want to know how effective your efforts are when engaging your target audience on LinkedIn. LinkedIn offers basic analytics that allows you to monitor and track how many visitors you get to your company page.

However, these analytics are not sophisticated enough to inform you of how effectively you are engaging your target audience. Despite this, on your main Company Page, you can see who has commented on your company updates and have otherwise engaged with your content.

Because there is limited analytics available, you will have to do your own sleuthing. Make time every day to engage in company networking. Make updates and check on previous updates to see what type of engagement they have received. By doing this, you will be able to see what types of updates are engaging your target audience and what isn't working. You can then adjust your updates accordingly. You should also make use of the analytics that go with your company website when tracking lead generation and any traffic your website receives from LinkedIn.

Getting Started

With all of this information at your fingertips, the time to start or revamp your LinkedIn marketing campaign is now. Setting up your Company Page is the beginning, so take the time to do it right. Once you have your page up and running, be consistent in posting your company updates and engaging with your followers. If you do this, you will see your number of followers grow and your level of engagement go through the virtual roof.

Making the Switch

"Going viral is not an outcome; it's a happening. Sometimes it happens; sometimes it doesn't. Just remember, fans are vanity and sales are sanity."
Lori Taylor

What you have learned in the preceding chapters will help you to utilize social media platforms to promote your brand and your company to the very best of your ability. Social media marketing truly will take your brand and your business to the next level, and in today's world, you simply will not succeed without some component of social media presence.

However, if your business has been run on more traditional forms of marketing, such as e-mail marketing, direct mail, and magazine and newspaper advertisements, then you will need to make the switch to a more social media-based marketing approach. This means that your entire business environment will change, and unless you are a one-person show in your business, you will have to bring your employees onboard.

There are a number of things that you will have to do to get your business social media ready. I will detail those here. This will not include the specifics of each platform as those are discussed in detail in the preceding chapters. Instead, this will be a broader discussion about how to plan for the shift, how to get employees onboard, and how company culture has to support the shift to social media marketing.

Creating a Social Media Marketing Plan

In order to help your business transition to the use of social media marketing, you will need to take a steady and consistent approach to the transformation. This will begin with the creation of a social media marketing plan that is tailored to your business. Let's take a look at this process in detail.

Objectives and Goals

You need to know precisely what you are trying to achieve with your SMM and how you are going to achieve it. Your SMM objectives will likely be in line with your overall marketing objectives. You might want to increase brand awareness, generate leads, increase traffic on your website and in your brick-and-mortar location, and ultimately increase your number of clients/customers. SMM will help you to achieve these objectives, but you have to set some solid SMM goals to do so. Use the SMART approach when setting SMM goals.

Specific: Ensure your goals are specific, that you know the Ws, as in Who, What, Where, Why, When, and How you will meet your goals.

Measurable: Set your goals such that you are able to see when you have reached those goals. These goals might be a certain number of followers, a certain number of retweets or repins, a certain amount of web traffic generated, or a certain number of leads generated. You will want to achieve these goals within a specified period of time.

Attainable: Be realistic when setting your SMM goals. You do not want to set a goal so high that it will be difficult to attain it. If you do this, then you are likely setting yourself up for failure. Setting a goal of reaching a million Twitter or Instagram followers in a year might be a bit too lofty, unless you happen to be Taylor Swift or Katy Perry. Perhaps 100,000 followers is a more reasonable goal.

Relevant: You want to be sure that the SMM goals that you set are relevant to your overall marketing and business objectives. It might be a worthy goal, but the timing might not be right. If the goal doesn't matter in the grand scheme of things, then you should scrap it so that you don't waste your time.

Timely: Not only should your goal have a deadline, but the deadline should be reasonable and the timeline should be able to be broken down into smaller milestones. Let's look at the goal of acquiring 100,000 followers within a year. You can break that down into quarters. This way you know you need to acquire 25,000 followers per quarter. If you aren't at 25,000 by the end of the first quarter, then you can make changes and adjust your course to pick-up the slack.

Perform a Social Media Audit
Setting goals is determining your destination, but in order to draw a map to get there, you will need to know your starting point. In other words, you will need to determine your current use of social media, the platforms your target market uses, and the social media presence of your competitors. Follow these steps to audit your social media presence:

1. Write down all the social media accounts/profiles your business owns.
2. Google any social media accounts for your business that are owned by other people/entities.
3. Determine the needs of each of your social media accounts/profiles and create a mission statement for each one of them. For instance, your mission for your LinkedIn account might be to improve your B2B networking and your Twitter mission could be to promote your company and industry news and updates.
4. Ensure that every social media profile is consistent in branding, including logos, cover photos, icons, bios, and descriptions.
5. Ensure that all passwords are centralized within your organization, such as being controlled by your IT department.

6. Establish procedures for adding new social media channels so that there is a set of criteria to meet and determine who will approve social media requests.

Once you have completed these steps, you will know about every account connected to your brand and company and you will be able to report fraudulent accounts not owned by you. The accounts you own can be updated or deleted as you see fit and you will be able to mold your social media presence into something that will benefit your brand.

Creating/Improving Social Media Accounts

Now that you know what accounts you have, what they contain, and what accounts you need to create to fill in the gaps, you can adjust current accounts and create new ones as you deem necessary to meet the objectives of your company. This will mean deciding which social media platforms are the best ones to help you meet the goals you set for SMM and your company objectives. If the social media profiles on those platforms already exist, then adjust them to create the presence you desire. If they do not exist, then you will have to build them from scratch. Either way, the preceding chapters of this book will help you to accomplish these goals.

Check Out the Competition

No marketing campaign or business can manage without knowing what the competition is up to. That is something that has not changed over the decades. It is wise to check out your direct competition to see what their social media presence is like. You might find that you are woefully behind or that you are one step ahead of the game. You might get inspiration for your own SMM campaign by seeing what the competition is doing.

When checking out the competition, you can see:

- How many followers/fans they have
- The types of content they post
- How they express or phrase their content
- The types of content that get the most response
- Where they might be lacking in content so that you can fill the gap
- How the target audience responds so that you can mimic their style in your own posts
- When the competition makes their posts
- When the target audience is responding to or engaging with those posts

Create a SMM Plan

Once you have reached this step, you have a basic social media profile on each of the platforms you deem necessary and you have a good idea of what your competition is up to and what you need to do to get ahead and succeed in reaching your SMM goals. Now you need to plan out your SMM strategy by determining the following:

- The type of content you will post
- Your target audience
- The frequency at which you will post
- Who will create and post the content
- How the content will be promoted

Essentially, you will need an editorial calendar to lay out the dates and times of day that you will post content and what content will be posted each of those times. Be sure to be careful in how you construct your content, whether it is in text or visual. You want to consider how you will present your content carefully. The spontaneity in your social media presence will come when you engage with your audience and respond to their questions, feedback, input, and concerns.

It is also important to ensure that all of your content and your posting schedule reflects the overall mission statement you have created for that social media platform. If you want to promote company culture, then at least half of your content should focus on that aspect of your business or brand. If your primary mission is to generate leads, then half or more of your content should focus on lead generation. If you are not sure what to post, then follow the rule of thirds:

- 1/3 of content promotes business, results in conversions, and generates a profit.
- 1/3 of content will focus on sharing content from the leaders in your industry.
- 1/3 of content focuses on personal interactions and building your brand.

Test, Evaluate, Adjust

Through the methods of SMM analysis we spoke about in the various chapters above, you will be able to see what is working and what isn't. You will then be able to adjust the course of your SMM campaign accordingly to ensure the best results. You can also ask your audience directly for their feedback on your efforts. A survey is a great way to accomplish this. The key to a successful SMM campaign is that it is dynamic and constantly changing. This means adjusting your content as needed and adding new platforms as they become available. It will also mean that as your goals and mission change, so too will the content that you post. Don't be afraid to adjust your plan and even start from scratch when necessary!

Social Media Policy

As with any other aspect of corporate operations, you will need solid policies around the implementation of SMM. You need to have a set of guidelines as to what employees are allowed to do and what they are NOT allowed to do. In other words, these are guidelines that set the expectations for what behavior is appropriate online and they might save you some difficulties down the road. They might also protect the company and individuals from facing potential legal issues in the future.

I won't go into great detail on creating a social media policy here, but I will include the basics of what to include. You will need to clearly prohibit the following:

- The sharing of confidential or proprietary company and client/customer information.
- The inclusion of content that is inflammatory or derogatory or can be construed as defaming an individual or entity.
- The posting of any photos or information that implies the individual or company has participated in illegal activities.

You must also be sure to include sections on the following:

- Transparency – how employees represent themselves and the company on social media platforms.
- Crisis management – how to deal with controversy and confrontation.
- Privacy – How employees can protect themselves and others when posting content.

- Compliance – Awareness of the regulatory bodies and governing principles by which the company must operate and how they affect a company's social media presence.
- Endorsement – Ensure there are clear guidelines around what the company does and does not endorse.

Getting Employees Onboard

Unless you operate a business in which you are by yourself, you will need to have employees to get onboard with your social media marketing strategy. Whether you have one employee or 100 employees, every single one of them will have to embrace the change with you or it won't be effective. The problem with getting a total company buy-in can happen at any level.

Sometimes it is the top-level executives that don't think the effort is worth the time it will take to implement the change. Sure, social media marketing is nearly cost-free in terms of financial investment, but in terms of the investment of time and effort, there is a fairly significant investment and sometimes the idea of tasking people with developing and running a SMM campaign is something of which upper management is skeptical.

Sometimes it is middle-management that doubts about whether developing and executing a SMM campaign is worth it. However, in the majority of cases, the problem facing companies is the fact that the employees of the company are not familiar enough with social media (a shock, I know!) to understand what it can do for the company and how they can play a part in making it a success.

If you don't already have every employee in the company accepting the shift to social media marketing, then you need to get everyone onboard now. There is no time to lose. There is no more leaving it in the hands of the marketing department (if you even have one of those) or putting it off until you have time and resources. It is now or never. The following are things you can do to ensure everyone buys into the SMM concept and does their part.

Establish a Leader

The leader might be you or it might be Joan in the marketing department. The point is that someone needs to coordinate the efforts of the company to get the SMM initiative off the ground. The person can be granted the title of CCO, Chief Content Officer, or CMO, Chief Marketing Officer. Essentially, you have to make it an official position and you have to be sure the person in that position understands what they need to do. What if it's just you? What if you have no employees? Well, then you have one more hat to wear and you must wear it well.

Educate

If you want to pull people into the concept of SMM, then you need to make it exciting. There should not be any mass e-mails sent out asking employees to write a blog article or asking everyone to Like the company Facebook page. Even if they do this stuff, it isn't going to make any SMM campaign fly.

You need to make every employee understand the power social media has and get them excited about it. The only way to really accomplish this is to hold an event. Anything that is worthy of an event must be exciting and worth their time and attention. You can host a "Social Media Conference" and require everyone to attend.

During the conference, you can spend the first half educating everyone on the different social media platforms and what social media can do for the company. You can also teach the employees how content marketing works to help promote a brand on social media. Use real-life examples of what is happening on social media. Bring it home to everyone just how powerful social media is.

Encourage Action

With all or most of your employees at the conference and understanding the power of social media, you then need to encourage people to take action. Prior to the conference, you will need to establish a plan of action that you can share with employees. This way, you can explain to them precisely what they can do to help the company with the SMM campaign.

For example, you might plan to use blogging as a major part of your SMM campaign. You can brainstorm with employees at the conference and pull together the most common questions and comments that you receive from customers or clients. These can be made into blog topics that can be assigned to the staff. Staff can also help with things like pinning content from projects they are working on, posting photos from events, or keeping up with industry news and sharing that on social media. You can have employees assigned to different platforms and have them devise a schedule of posts. There are really many ways to approach this so that everyone can get involved and excited.

Social Media Newsletter

Once you have had your conference, you have the ball rolling but now you need to maintain the momentum. A social media newsletter is a great way to accomplish this. The CCO/CMO is responsible for this newsletter, which needs to come out on a regular and consistent basis. There are so many things that you can include in a newsletter focused on the company's social media efforts, such as:

- Providing numbers, including the increase in website traffic, sales, and leads that came from social media marketing efforts.

- Special mentions of blogs, articles, or other types of posts made by employees.
- Examples of social media content that made a direct impact on sales or another aspect of the company.
- Examples of positive comments and testimonials left by customers and followers.
- An opportunity for employees to leave comments and feedback.

The whole point of the newsletter is to ensure that the importance of the SMM campaign is continually reinforced. This will keep employees excited about participating for the long-term and it will have a huge positive impact on company culture.

Ongoing Training and Education

As you can well imagine, social media is constantly evolving and changing. For this reason, there absolutely must be an ongoing effort to train and educate employees. The popularity and use of social media platforms comes and goes. New social media platforms pop up all the time. Demographics of social media platforms change over time. If you and your employees are not keeping up-to-date, then you won't be able to make the necessary changes to your SMM campaign and it will cease to be effective. There are many aspects of social media marketing in which you can train your employees, such as:

- Video production
- Image creation
- Developing contests and surveys
- Writing short posts
- Determining the best content to pin

When all is said and done, if you follow these guidelines, you will gain the commitment that you need from everyone in your organization. Together, you can create a SMM campaign that will ensure your business is a success and remains one for years to come.

Conclusion

Congratulations! You have reached the end of this social media marketing book. However, you are just at the beginning of your SMM journey, one that will take you, your brand, and your company to new heights of success. I hope that as you have read this, you have already begun to think about what social media platforms will work best for your brand and that you have started making plans. But there are two things that must happen before anything else will fall into place that you must do before you can really embark on this SMM journey...

1. You absolutely must accept that change is inevitable.
2. You have to embrace that change.

If you do not do both of these things, then your business and your brand will stagnate. You will get left behind in the marketing and technological dark ages. There is simply no room in the future of business for any brand that is not represented on social media. It is that simple.

With this in mind, remember these words...

"These days, social media waits for no one. If you're LATE for the party, you'll probably be covered by all the noise and you might not be able to get your voice across. It could only mean that if you want to be heard by the crowd, you have to be fast; and on social media, that means you have to be REALLY fast."
Aaron Lee

Good luck with your social media marketing endeavors, and most importantly, have fun along the journey!

CPSIA information can be obtained
at www.ICGtesting.com
Printed in the USA
FSHW021249021020
74394FS

9 781530 429769